Nikki
Godnyuk

# GENESIS

## *Finding Our Roots*

Ruth Beechick

Book Design: McCallum Design Co.
Illustrations: Michael Denman

**MOTT MEDIA**

ABOVE : The Great Architect of the Universe. This view of God was painted in a hand-illustrated Bible in France in the 1200s. The compass is large, like those in the Middle Ages. God traces out the limits of the universe. The earth is still without form, the firmament shows between the waters, and the heavenly lights can be seen.

© 1997 by Arrow Press

© 2016 by Mott Media L.L.C.

For information about other Mott Media publications visit our website at www. mottmedia.com.

Printed by Color House Graphics, Grand Rapids, Michigan, USA

ISBN-13: 978-0-88062-139-7        ISBN-10: 0-88062-139-7

# *Contents*

"And there was light." Bible illustration by French artist Gustave Doré, with engraving by H. Pisan. In 1866 this Boble was published in English, and Doré's energetic style became much admired. Several are shown in this book.

# *Reason for this Book*

The first chapters of Genesis are no doubt the oldest writings in the world, as we show in some of the studies included here, and their importance cannot be exceeded. The basis for mankind's thinking is set in these writings.

These writings answer all the major questions that philosophers wrestle with. Who are we? Where did we come from? Why are we here? Where are we going? Is there a God? What is He like? The true answers found in Genesis form the basic world view of informed and thinking Christians. Our view of these fundamental questions affects all our thinking, and only a right view will produce right thinking.

Our answers to these questions not only affect our thinking, they also affect the way we live. And society's answers affect the way our society lives. Why is Western society crumbling? It's because we have cast out the book of Genesis. We no longer believe that life comes from God, so we do not value life but practice abortion, euthanasia, and suicide instead. We no longer believe that man is made in the image of God, so animal "rights" can be higher than man's. We no longer believe in God, so we ignore His laws. We no longer believe in the Creator, so we worship His creation rather than Him.

Our society desperately needs to find Genesis again. Studying this book will help with that need. If you lead your family or class through these studies, you will give them a solid foundation for all subsequent learning, the basis for clear thinking, the true principles against which all important issues in life should be judged. The cure for fuzzy thinking is knowledge of the Genesis principles.

A great literature professor, Northrup Frye, said, ". . . the Bible forms the lowest stratum in the teaching of literature. It should be taught so early and so thoroughly that it sinks straight to the bottom of the mind, where everything that comes along later can settle on it." The Bible is the foundation for literature—and history. And the foundation of the Bible is its early chapters. Your child's education can stand on no firmer foundation than this.

The roots of mankind are preserved in these ancient writings, and civilized man is on his way to losing this precious heritage. We are losing the history of our origins, not by fire as with the Alexendrian library, but by neglect and distortion of ancient truths, as well as by outright banning of and hostility to the Scriptures.

A good education today often means ability to find and manipulate information by computer. This is called the "information age" and we demand more and newer and faster information, as though information is education. But education must begin with first principles and the right thinking that flows from them. Genesis 1-11 contains what God and our earliest forefathers set down in writing for us. We must preserve it in the minds and hearts of our children.

This book is to help with that worthy and important goal.

# *The Organization of this Book*

These studies are organized, first, around the Scripture itself. Secondly, several fields of study are integrated into the six units.

An important field integrated here is theology. Theology used to be called "the queen of the sciences," but today it has disappeared from general education. These studies help to put it back. Theology doesn't have to be scary for the student; it is simply learning about basic ideas such as what God can do and what He is like, or where mankind came from and what his purpose is in this life.

Other fields included in the units are: history, geography, literature, art, linguistics, science, and even a bit of arithmetic.

The Scripture is divided into six units here. A detailed explanation of why and how the six divisions are made is given in the Scripture Study section of Unit II. Each of the six units contains four sections as listed below.

## 1. Scripture Text

Each unit opens with the Scripture portion needed for the unit. This is given in King James Version because of its universality, but students may use their own favorite versions instead.

## 2. Scripture Study

Following the Scripture text are suggestions for study which require no additional books, only the Scripture itself.

## 3. Topic Study

These topics in each unit expand on and relate to the Scripture in various ways, particularly with literary and historical emphases. Information needed for these short studies is included in this book. You can select from these according to your purpose. Some fit well into Sunday school use, along with the Scripture study. Others fit better into family or homeschool settings or as references for school reports. Brief helps for answers to the Topic Study questions are found on pages 120-123.

## 4. Further Study

These projects in each unit often reach beyond the present book. Readings in other books are suggested, as are writing and speaking assignments, map and chart work, and some arithmetic.

# Unit I

## God's Book of Creation

"And God said, Let the earth bring forth the living creature after his kind, cattle, and creeping thing, and beast of the earth after his kind: and it was so" (Genesis 1:24).

Creation of the World, by artist Bernard Picart, with engraving work done by Phil. a Gunst. From a manuscript of 1732 called *Metamorphoses*, written in Latin and English. This shows vigorous movement not only in the figure of God, but also in the sky and sea and trees and the living creatures. The artist may be showing the process of bringing order out of the formless and empty earth that was made in the beginning.

# *Scripture Text*

## *God's Book of Creation*

**Genesis 1:1** In the beginning God created the heaven and the earth. **2** And the earth was without form, and void; and darkness *was* upon the face of the deep. And the Spirit of God moved upon the face of the waters. **3** And God said, Let there be light: and there was light. **4** And God saw the light, that *it was* good: and God divided the light from the darkness. **5** And God called the light Day, and the darkness he called Night. And the evening and the morning were the first day. **6** And God said, Let there be a firmament in the midst of the waters, and let it divide the waters from the waters. **7** And God made the firmament, and divided the waters which *were* under the firmament from the waters which *were* above the firmament: and it was so. **8** And God called the firmament Heaven. And the evening and the morning were the second day. **9** And God said, Let the waters under the heaven be gathered together unto one place, and let the dry *land* appear: and it was so. **10** And God called the dry *land* Earth; and the gathering together of the waters called he Seas: and God saw that *it was* good. **11** And God said, Let the earth bring forth grass, the herb yielding seed, *and* the fruit tree yielding fruit after his kind, whose seed *is* in itself, upon the earth: and it was so. **12** And the earth brought forth grass, *and* herb yielding seed after his kind, and the tree yielding fruit, whose seed *was* in itself, after his kind: and God saw that it *was* good. **13** And the evening and the morning were the third day. **14** And God said, Let there be lights in the firmament of the heaven to divide the day from the night; and let them be for signs, and for seasons, and for days, and years: **15** And let them be for lights in the firmament of the heaven to give light upon the earth: and it was so. **16** And God made two great lights; the greater light to rule the day, and the lesser light to rule the night: *he made* the stars also. **17** And God set them in the firmament of the heaven to give light upon the earth, **18** And to rule over the day and over the night, and to divide the light from the darkness: and God saw that it *was good.* **19** And the evening and the morning were the fourth day. **20** And God said, Let the waters bring forth abundantly the moving creature that hath life, and fowl *that* may fly above the earth in the open firmament of heaven. **21** And God created great whales, and every living creature that moveth, which the waters brought forth abundantly, after their kind, and every winged fowl after his kind: and God saw that *it was* good. **22** And God blessed them, saying, Be fruitful, and multiply, and fill the waters in the seas, and let fowl multiply in the earth. **23** And the evening and the morning were the fifth day. **24** And God said, Let the earth bring forth the living creature after his kind, cattle, and creeping thing, and beast of the earth after his kind: and it was so. **25** And God made the beast of the earth after his kind, and cattle after their kind, and every thing that creepeth upon the earth after his kind: and God saw that it *was good.* **26** And God said, Let us make man in our image, after our likeness: and let them have dominion over the fish of the sea, and over the fowl of the air, and over the cattle, and over all the earth, and over every creeping thing that creepeth upon the earth. **27** So God created man in his *own* image, in the image of God created he him; male and female created he them. **28** And God blessed them, and God said unto them, Be fruitful, and multiply, and replenish the earth, and subdue it: and have dominion over the fish of the sea, and over the fowl of the air, and over every living thing that moveth upon the earth. **29** And God said, Behold, I have given you every herb bearing seed, which is upon the face of all the earth, and every tree, in the which *is* the fruit of a tree yielding seed; to you it shall be for meat. **30** And to every beast of the earth, and to every fowl of the air, and to every thing that creepeth upon the earth, wherein *there is* life, I *have given* every green herb for meat: and it was so. **31** And God saw every thing that he had made, and, behold, *it was* very good. And the evening and the morning were the sixth day. **2:1** Thus the heavens and the earth were finished, and all the host of them. **2** And on the seventh day God ended his work which he had made; and he rested on the seventh day from all his work which he had made. **3** And God blessed the seventh day, and sanctified it: because that in it he had rested from all his work which God created and made. **4** These *are* the generations of the heavens and of the earth when they were created . . .

(See picture from hand copied Hebrew Bible on p.68)

# Scripture Study

**Read.** "God's Book of Creation" is no doubt the oldest book in the world. Either God wrote the words himself, as He wrote the ten commandments, or He told Adam the words to write. Then the book was passed down until it reached Moses. Moses included it in the book of Genesis, and it was passed on down to us. So now we can read this most ancient book, by the Creator himself, and learn the true story of creation. Take time to read the words of God's book from the copy given here or from the translation of your choice. Has your family ever read this aloud?

**Mark** the following creation information in your Bible or in this book or on a photocopy. These markings will help you carry out other projects in this study.

a) Find where it says "And the evening and the morning were the first day," and draw a line below that to separate the first and second days. Draw similar lines after each day from 2 through 6.

b) In the margins, number the sections you made to show the six days of creation.

c) For the six days of creation (Genesis 1:1-31) circle the word *created* everywhere you find it. You should find three. Number them in order. You could circle these numerals to separate them from the six-day numerals. Or you could use Roman numerals. The word *create* in Hebrew is *bara* (baw RAW) and it means to create something out of nothing.

**Tell** what happened on one or more of the creation days.

**Memorize** verse 1:1, the oldest words in the oldest book in the world. Only two beliefs about the origin of the universe are possible. Either matter is eternal and somehow formed into a universe by itself or a Supreme Being is eternal and created the universe. This beautiful statement at the beginning of our Bible tells the true origin of all things.

For this and other memory verses, use your favorite translation of the Bible.

# Topic Study

## Dragons

Verse 1:21 begins, "And God created great *tanniyn*." The Hebrew word *tanniyn* (tan NEEN) means dragons, but the King James translators wrote *whales*, perhaps because that was the biggest real creature they knew in those days. Elsewhere in the Bible they translated it *dragons*. For some examples, see Deuteronomy 32:33, Jeremiah 14:6, and Micah 1:8. This word is used about 25 times in the Bible.

Ancient people called them dragons and we call them dinosaurs. The translators could have written *dinosaurs* if they had had such a word then. But they didn't. The word wasn't invented until the 1800s. Somebody translating the verse now could say, "And God created great dinosaurs." You will find more on dragons in the dinosaur topic of Unit IV.

Do you think dinosaurs look like dragons?
On which day of creation week did God create the great
    sea creatures?
Why didn't the King James translators call those dinosaurs?

## Create

Only three times in Genesis 1 do we find the word *create* (Hebrew *bara*). These are in verses 1, 21 and 27. In other verses God made something, or told something to come forth. But only these three times did He create.

So the three *bara*'s are worth looking at closely. Verse 1 tells of God's original creation of all matter and energy. He made the universe out of nothing (Hebrews 11:3). Following that original creation, came light, land, water, sky, plants and heavenly lights, not *created* but *made* from the original matter and energy created on the first day.

The second *bara* creation happened on the fifth day when God created living creatures for the sea and sky. Their bodies were made from matter that God created on the first day, but now He created life for them out of nothing. The next day the earth brought forth land animals at God's word, and life was already available for them. God did not create animal life again.

The third *bara* creation occurred later that sixth day. God created humans—male and female. Animal life would not do for humans. It took a new act of creation to make man in the image of God. This Scripture clearly shows that humans are a different order of being than animals. It refutes the evolutionist idea that animals evolved into humans.

In summary, the three acts of *bara* creation are:
    1) matter and energy;
    2) animal life;
    3) human life.

The word *bara* occurs 54 times in the Bible and practically always refers to creation by God, out of nothing. When we talk about people being creative, we mean something less than *bara*.

What can you do that animals cannot do?
Make a chart in three parts, showing what God made

after each *bara* act of creation.
Find out what your pastor says about the image of God in
    humans. Or find something about it in a book.
Write a paragraph which explains that humans are a higher
    kind of being than animals.

(Brief helps for answers to the Topic Study questions
are found on pages 120-123.)

# Day

The word *yom* (YOME), day, first appears in verse 5. A rule in Bible study says that the first use of a word shows what it means there and in all later uses, unless the context gives it a different meaning.

This rule applies not only in Bible study, but everywhere. Good writers don't carelessly switch meanings of a word, but their context makes clear which meaning they want.

So it is important to see that in verse 5 *yom* means the light time, and it also means the full 24-hour cycle of evening and morning. We commonly use *day* in these two related ways, to speak of a full calendar day and of the light part of the day.

According to the Bible study rule, then, that's what *yom* means in the Bible unless the context shows it must mean something else. *Yom* is repeated throughout chapter 1, always with the literal meaning of a solar day. We can't mistake God's meaning when He says, "the evening and the morning were the third day." "Evening and morning" makes it clear. And if that weren't enough, the numbers (third, fourth, etc.) emphasize it again. Everywhere in the Bible when *yom* is used with a number it means literal solar days.

A researcher once wrote to nine leading university professors of Hebrew and asked them what *yom* means in Genesis 1. He asked which of these three meanings it has.

1. day as commonly understood
2. an age
3. either a day or an age without preference

Seven professors responded and all seven said it should be translated day as commonly understood. The professors do not necessarily believe the Bible, but they agreed that the Bible says these are literal days.

Yet some people say that the days in Genesis 1 are long ages of time. There is no Bible reason for that belief. The main reason is that people believe evolutionists. And evolutionists need long, long ages of time for humans to accidentally evolve. They have no evidence that it happened, but at least they can fit the theory better into long ages than into six days. According to researcher John R. Howitt (1981), Russell Grigg gives additional linguistic proofs that this is a literal solar day in "How Long Were the Days of Genesis 1?" in *Creation ex nihilo*, Vol. 19 No. 1.

> Write out a Bible study rule about the meaning of Bible words.
>
> Using this rule, what is the usual meaning of *day* in the Bible?
>
> Using this rule, what is the meaning of *create (bara)* in the Bible?

# Origin of the Week

Why do we have a seven-day week? In practically all places and all times people have observed a seven-day week, and this is a puzzle to those who do not believe the Bible. They can't figure out how and why the week got started.

It's easy to see that the month is connected with the moon and the year is connected with the sun, but the week is not connected with any sky signs. Nor does it seem to come from anything else in nature. Yet it has existed for thousands of years.

Dictator Stalin in the Soviet Union tried to erase the memory of the seven-day week because he wanted to erase all religious memory in his citizens. In Russian language, Sunday is called Ressurrection Day, and Stalin didn't want that reminder every seven days. So he instituted a ten-day week and called the days simply by numbers. It turned out that people couldn't work nine days with one day of rest. The experiment fell apart, and Russians returned to the age-old week of seven days. Other attempts to change the week have also failed, and the week has existed now for almost 6000 years.

Bible believers know the answer to the puzzling question. The seven-day period originated that first week in history, and every week that goes by reminds us of that creation week. God himself spoke this reminder from Mount Sinai. And He wrote the commandment with his own finger on tablets of stone.

"Two months are olive harvest. Two months are planting grain . . ." A Hebrew schoolboy learns an ancient calendar poem.

"Remember the sabbath day, to keep it holy. Six days shalt thou labour, and do all thy work: But the seventh day is the sabbath of the Lord thy God. . . . For in six days the Lord made heaven and earth, the sea, and all that in them is, and rested the seventh day" (from Exodus 20:8-11).

Some Bible scholars say that the number seven stands for spiritual perfection or completion. We see this first in Genesis, when God rested on the seventh day and His work of creation was completed. Later in Revelation we see seven candlesticks which were the seven churches (1:20). Then follow the seven seals, seven trumpets and seven plagues of God's judgment. People who are interested in studying numbers find still more sevens in the rest of the Bible.

A golden candlestick with seven lights burned in the Tabernacle and the Temple (Exodus 25:31-37).

What heavenly body is the year tied to?
(After creation the year may have been an exact 360-day cycle, which was disrupted at some disaster, such as Noah's Flood.)

What heavenly body is the month tied to?

What historical event is the week tied to?

## The Rest of the Bible

We can read about God's creation not only in Genesis, but also throughout the rest of the Bible. Here are a few examples.

In the time of Moses, **God** wrote these words on stone with His own finger.

". . . in six days the Lord made heaven and earth, the sea, and all that in them is, and rested the seventh day: wherefore the Lord blessed the sabbath day, and hallowed it" (Exodus 20:11).

In another book **Moses** wrote of "the day that God created man upon the earth" (Deuteronomy 4:32).

In the time when the Israelites lived in their land, a **psalmist** sang, "By the word of the Lord were the heavens made; and all the host of them by the breath of his mouth. . . . For he spake, and it was done" (Psalm 33:6 and 9a). Other psalms, too, tell about creation.

The prophet **Isaiah** wrote, "Thus saith the Lord that created the heavens; God himself that formed the earth and made it" (Isaiah 45:18).

**Jesus** believed the Genesis creation story. Once when some Pharisees asked a question, He said, "Have ye not read, that he which made them at the beginning made them male and female" (Matthew 19:4).

The apostle **John** wrote, "All things were made by him; and without him was not anything made that was made" (John 1:3).

**Paul** wrote of Christ, "For by him were all things created, that are in heaven, and that are in earth, visible and invisible, whether they be thrones, or dominions, or principalities, or powers: all things were created by him and for him" (Colossians 1:16).

**Every New Testament writer** referred to or quoted from the book of Genesis. Dr. Henry Morris has counted at least 200 of these references in the New Testament, and 68 of them directly refer to the first eleven chapters of Genesis, which tell of creation and the first sin and other beginnings. (*The Genesis Record*, page 21.)

> Do later Bible books agree with the first Bible book that God created everything?
>
> How many New Testament writers can you name who used something from Genesis in their writings?
>
> What could you tell a person who says he believes in Jesus but thinks the Genesis story of creation is not literally true?

## Basic World Views

The big questions of life are about God, the world, and the people. All through history men have wondered about the big questions, but even a child can find answers in this little book from God, the oldest book in the world. Below are some basic ideas that form our world view.

**God is a person.** That means God thinks and speaks and acts with plan and purpose. Theologians call Him a "personal God." They don't mean that God is yours or mine, giving us personal attention. God does give us personal attention, of course, but theologians mean something greater—that God is a person, not just a force.

**God is one God.** This creation story sounds pure, simple and straight-forward, a contrast to heathen stories of the fightings and matings of multiple gods. In the phrase "Let us make," we have an early hint of the trinity that later Scriptures clarify: three persons, but only one God. Theologians call Him the triune (TRI yune or tri YUNE) God. Triune means "three-in-one."

**God is the Creator.** He is above, outside of and separate from His creation. Theologians say God is "transcendent" (tran SEN dent).

An opposite belief holds that the creation itself somehow is God. Trees, animals, people and everything in the universe are all supposed to be parts of one big whole, which began by itself and guides its own destiny. Some people call this wholeness *God*. Ancient pagans believed this. Some New Agers and other religionists today believe this. Also evolutionists, though they don't use the word *God*, believe essentially the same—that matter has within itself the powers of creation. This seems to be the dominant view even in the "Christian" West.

But God's book tells a different story. It clearly shows that God is a person, thinking, planning, creating, speaking, evaluating, blessing. He is transcendent to His creation.

**The world is real and the human mind can know it.** This sounds so simple to Bible believers that it seems hardly worth mentioning, but many philosophers and religionists do not agree at all. And this truth is immensely important to science. Science did not develop far while the world was under the sway of pagan religions. But when biblical thinking spread in the western world, modern science could be born. "Christianity is the mother of science," wrote philosopher Bertrand Russell. He could see the connection even though he was not a Christian himself.

Why did Christianity give birth to science? Because Christians believed in creation by a rational God—that is, a God who thinks and reasons. Such a God would make a rational universe. It would be unified, since it came from one mind. Its laws of cause and effect could be discovered by people, because they have reasoning minds too, being made in the image of God. This world view forms the foundation of modern science.

In medieval times people did not investigate the world for themselves. They just took the words of an authority, mostly Aristotle, and believed those instead. In modern times a good many scientists do not believe in the Creator God. Some, in fact, try to show that the world could come into being without God. And all the while they work according to

> medieval: (pronounced *me de EE val*) refers to the Middle Ages in European history, which is from the fall of the Roman Empire to the Italian Renaissance, about A.D. 500 to about A.D. 1450.

biblical principles that the world is real and unified, with orderly laws, and their minds can know the nature of the world.

> Tell one or more truths we learn about God from this book of creation.
>
> Tell something we can learn about humans from this book of creation.
>
> Tell something important we learn about the world from this book of creation.

# Myths of Creation

Many of the world's myths contain memories of the creation week. Pagan myths scramble the true story, and they add false gods, yet we can see bits of the original story in them.

In the original story, God first created the earth without form. Then He separated Day from Night, and Heaven from Earth (1:4-8).

The event of separating earth and sky appears in myths all over the world. To illustrate, here are two stories from two lands far apart from each other.

## Greece

Out of Chaos came Mother Earth. She gave birth to Father Sky, whose name was Uranus (YUR a nuhs). Uranus loved Mother Earth, so he showered rain and sunshine down upon her to give birth to flowers and trees and birds and all kinds of animals. He filled her rivers and seas with life.

But Uranus did not love all the sons of Mother Earth. Some he sent to the underworld. Mother Earth resented this, so she begged seven of her sons to push Uranus away. The sons struggled to do that, and the youngest son made a sickle of flint from a high peak. With that he wounded Uranus enough that he retreated to the outermost parts of the universe.

And that is how earth and sky were separated.

## Maori (MAH re) of New Zealand

Father Sky, whose name was Rangi, and Mother Earth embraced each other in love. In time, their children grew tired of the continuing darkness, so they consulted together about what to do. The Father of Human Beings suggested killing both parents. But the Father of Forests said, "Let us push our parents apart. Then we will still have Mother Earth for our support and Father Sky to care for us from above."

After much discussion, they voted to do as the Father of Forests suggested. So the Father of Cultivated Foods tried first, pushing with all his might, but he could not push his father away. Next tried the Father of Fish and the Father of Wild Foods, both without success. Even the Father of Human Beings could not push his father away.

Finally, the Father of Forests placed his head firmly against Mother Earth. Then he doubled up his legs and set the soles of his feet against Father Heaven.

"What are you doing?" asked his parents. "How dare you show such disrespect to your parents?"

But the Father of Forests slowly straightened out his back and stretched his long legs and pushed Father Sky away. Suddenly light came.

And that is how earth and sky were separated.

(See Gate of a Maori village on page 67)

Some scholars think that peoples of the world invented myths from their own imaginations to explain the beginnings of the world. How much chance do you think there is that the Greeks and the Maori could both have invented such similar stories?

Other scholars think that similarities in the stories are evidence that they came from a single source, when traced back far enough. Can you explain why this theory makes sense?

# *Further Study*

(This section in each unit includes projects and activities, some of
which reach beyond this book and require research from other sources.)

**1. Correlated Readings.** Two correlated books can be used throughout
these studies, as optional supplementary reading. The first book listed below
is a narrative by Ruth Beechick. The second, by Henry Morris, is a verse-by-
verse commentary with emphasis on scientific information for advanced students and adults. Both are available from bookstores. For Unit I, the suggested
readings are:

a) *Adam and His Kin*, chapter 1.

b) *The Genesis Record*, pages 37 to 81.

**2. Science Textbooks.** Do you have books that say something about how
the world began or how life began? Compare what they say with what the
Bible says.

**3. Other Readings.** Books on creation science will add to this study.
Many excellent books are available and more are appearing all the time
through the creationist organizations and publishers. (See bibliography for
some book suggestions.) Some suggested topics are:

a) *Fossils.* Do fossils show any gradual change from one kind to another,
as evolutionists would like? Or do they provide a record of definite kinds as
described in Genesis 1?

b) *Genetics.* Mendel's (MEN duhl) laws of inheritance show that variations
result from different combinations of genes, but there are never any new
genes. Thus there is a limit to variations that we can breed. For instance, we
can breed different varieties of dogs, but dogs can never become horses. The
variations are sometimes used as evidence that evolution occurs. But genetics
really provides better evidence that plants and animals are each made after its
own kind. Compare what school textbooks and creationist books say on the
topic of genetics.

c) *Upper and lower waters.* How did God divide the waters (1:6, 7)? Did
He put some in a vapor canopy surrounding the earth beyond the atmosphere?
And did He put some below a firm crust of earth? Dr. Larry Vardiman and
other prominent scientists are working out details of the canopy theory. How
much water was up there? How did it affect earth's climate? What was the
world like before Noah's Flood? Watch for books telling the interesting work
of these scientists.

**4. Writing.** Any of the following topics can be used for writing assignments or for discussions, or both. Discussions help you prepare for writing.
Discussion leaders and participants can try to raise questions that require

thinking of more reasons or more information about the topic. Afterward, the writing is easier.

a) Atheists believe there is no God. Write what you would like to tell an atheist about creation. You could argue that stars and people and the world couldn't just get here by themselves. The wonderful creation means there must be a Creator.

b) Write what you would tell a humanist, who believes that humans are the greatest beings. You may want to explain that humans are creatures of the great Creator God. Use information from God's book.

c) Write what you would tell an evolutionist, who believes that matter existed eternally and that life arose spontaneously from that matter and gradually developed into the living creatures we now know.

d) Write a poem of praise to the Creator. Hebrew poems often have a pattern of saying each thought twice. For instance, Psalm 148:2, 3 says:

> Praise ye him, all his angels:
> Praise ye him, all his hosts.

> Praise ye him, sun and moon:
> Praise him, all ye stars of light.

To make a creation poem, you can write out a part of Psalm 8, 19, 104 or 148 in couplets as shown above. Or make up your own poem. Or instead of a poem, write a prayer to God in prose form.

**5. Six-Day Chart.** Make a chart showing what was created or made on each of the six days. Or make this in the form of a booklet.

Here's a question to think about while you study your chart. What would happen between the third and the fourth day if there had been a long period of time between these events instead of just one day?

Ornament on the ceiling of York Minster. The cock and owl represent day and night.

> *Bless the Lord, you nights and days;*
> *Lift up his name forever.*
>
> *Bless the Lord, you light and darkness;*
> *Lift up his name forever.*
>
> *Bless the Lord, O sun and moon;*
> *Praise his name forever.*
>
> *O all you works of the Lord,*
> *Praise his name forever.*

(Lines adapted from "A Song of Creation," found in the Apocrypha and various later prayer books. Compare with Psalm 148 and with the hymn "All Creatures of Our God and King," by St. Francis of Assisi.)

# Unit II

## Book of Adam

". . . and he placed at the east of the garden of Eden Cherubims, and a flaming sword which turned every way, to keep the way of the tree of life" (Genesis 3:24).

A Bible illustration by Gustave Doré, published first in France in 1865 and published in many editions since. Doré's Bible illustrations became known for their vitality and realism, and for their faithfulness to the meaning of the Scripture. These cherubims are four as in Ezekiel 10 and have horses as do the spirits in Zechariah 6.

# *Scripture Text*

## *Book of Adam*

**Genesis 2:4b** . . . in the day that the Lord God made the earth and the heavens, **5** And every plant of the field before it was in the earth, and every herb of the field before it grew: for the Lord God had not caused it to rain upon the earth, and *there was* not a man to till the ground. **6** But there went up a mist from the earth, and watered the whole face of the ground. **7** And the Lord God formed man *of* the dust of the ground, and breathed into his nostrils the breath of life; and man became a living soul. **8** And the Lord God planted a garden eastward in Eden; and there he put the man whom he had formed. **9** And out of the ground made the Lord God to grow every tree that is pleasant to the sight, and good for food; the tree of life also in the midst of the garden, and the tree of knowledge of good and evil. **10** And a river went out of Eden to water the garden; and from thence it was parted, and became into four heads. **11** The name of the first *is* Pison: that *is* it which compasseth the whole land of Havilah, where *there* is gold; **12** And the gold of that land *is* good: there *is* bdellium and the onyx stone. **13** And the name of the second river *is* Gihon: the same *is* it that compasseth the whole land of Ethiopia. **14** And the name of the third river *is* Hiddekel: that *is* it which goeth toward the east of Assyria. And the fourth river *is* Euphrates. **15** And the Lord God took the man, and put him into the garden of Eden to dress it and to keep it. **16** And the Lord God commanded the man, saying, Of every tree of the garden thou mayest freely eat: **17** But of the tree of the knowledge of good and evil, thou shalt not eat of it: for in the day that thou eatest thereof thou shalt surely die. **18** And the Lord God said, *It is* not good that the man should be alone; I will make him an help meet for him. **19** And out of the ground the Lord God formed every beast of the field, and every fowl of the air; and brought *them* unto Adam to see what he would call them: and whatsoever Adam called every living creature, that *was* the name thereof. **20** And Adam gave names to all cattle, and to the fowl of the air, and to every beast of the field; but for Adam there was not found an help meet for him. **21** And the Lord God caused a deep sleep to fall upon Adam, and he slept: and he took one of his ribs, and closed up the flesh instead thereof; **22** And the rib, which the Lord God had taken from man, made he a woman, and brought her unto the man. **23** And Adam said, This *is* now bone of my bones, and flesh of my flesh: she shall be called Woman, because she was taken out of Man. **24** Therefore shall a man leave his father and his mother, and shall cleave unto his wife: and they shall be one flesh. **25** And they were both naked, the man and his wife, and were not ashamed. **3:1** Now the serpent was more subtil than any beast of the field which the Lord God had made. And he said unto the woman, Yea, hath God said, Ye shall not eat of every tree of the garden? **2** And the woman said unto the serpent, We may eat of the fruit of the trees of the garden: **3** But of the fruit of the tree which *is* in the midst of the garden, God hath said, Ye shall not eat of it, neither shall ye touch it, lest ye die. **4** And the serpent said unto the woman, Ye shall not surely die: **5** For God doth know that in the day ye eat thereof, then your eyes shall be opened, and ye shall be as gods, knowing good and evil. **6** And when the woman saw that the tree *was* good for food, and that it *was* pleasant to the eyes, and a tree to be desired to make *one* wise, she took of the fruit thereof, and did eat, and gave also unto her husband with her; and he did eat. **7** And the eyes of them both were opened, and they knew that they *were* naked; and they sewed fig leaves together, and made themselves aprons. **8** And they heard the voice of the Lord God walking in the garden in the cool of the day: and Adam and his wife hid themselves from the presence of the Lord God amongst the trees of the garden. **9** And the Lord God called unto Adam, and said unto him, Where *art* thou? **10** And he said, I heard thy voice in the garden, and I was afraid, because I *was* naked; and I hid myself. **11** And he said, Who told thee that thou *wast* naked? Hast thou eaten of the tree, whereof I commanded thee that thou shouldest not eat? **12** And the man said, The woman whom thou gavest *to be* with me, she gave me of the tree, and I did eat. **13** And the Lord God said unto the woman, What *is* this *that* thou hast done? And the woman said, The serpent beguiled me, and I did eat. **14** And the Lord God said unto the serpent, Because thou hast done this, thou *art* cursed above all cattle, and above every beast of the field; upon thy belly shalt thou go, and dust shalt thou eat all the days of thy life: **15** And I will put enmity between thee and the woman, and between thy seed and her seed; it shall bruise thy head, and thou shalt bruise his heel. **16** Unto the woman he said, I will greatly multiply thy sorrow and thy conception; in sorrow thou shalt bring forth children; and thy desire *shall be* to thy husband, and he shall rule over thee. **17** And unto Adam he said, Because thou hast hearkened unto the voice of thy wife, and hast eaten of the tree, of which I commanded thee, saying, Thou shalt not eat of it: cursed *is* the ground for thy sake; in sorrow shalt thou eat *of* it all the days of thy life; **18** Thorns also and thistles shall it bring forth to thee; and thou shalt eat the herb of the field; **19** In the sweat of thy face shalt thou eat bread, till thou return unto the ground; for out of it wast thou taken: for dust thou *art*, and unto dust shalt thou return. **20** And Adam called his wife's name Eve; because she was the mother of all living. **21** Unto Adam also and to his wife did the Lord God make coats of skins, and clothed them. **22** And the Lord God said, Behold, the man is become as one of us, to know good and evil: and now, lest he put forth his hand, and take also of the tree of life, and eat, and live for ever: **23** Therefore the Lord God sent him forth from the garden of Eden, to till the ground from whence he was taken. **24** So he drove out the man; and he placed at the east of the garden of Eden

Cherubims, and a flaming sword which turned every way, to keep the way of the tree of life. **4:1** And Adam knew Eve his wife; and she conceived, and bare Cain, and said, I have gotten a man from the Lord. **2** And she again bare his brother Abel. And Abel was a keeper of sheep, but Cain was a tiller of the ground. **3** And in process of time it came to pass, that Cain brought of the fruit of the ground an offering unto the Lord. **4** And Abel, he also brought of the firstlings of his flock and of the fat thereof. And the Lord had respect unto Abel and to his offering: **5** But unto Cain and to his offering he had not respect. And Cain was very wroth, and his countenance fell. **6** And the Lord said unto Cain, Why art thou wroth? and why is thy countenance fallen? **7** If thou doest well, shalt thou not be accepted? and if thou doest not well, sin lieth at the door. And unto thee *shall be* his desire, and thou shalt rule over him. **8** And Cain talked with Abel his brother: and it came to pass, when they were in the field, that Cain rose up against Abel his brother, and slew him. **9** And the Lord said unto Cain, Where *is* Abel thy brother? And he said, I know not: *Am* I my brother's keeper? **10** And he said, What hast thou done? the voice of thy brother's blood crieth unto me from the ground. **11** And now *art* thou cursed from the earth, which hath opened her mouth to receive thy brother's blood from thy hand; **12** When thou tillest the ground, it shall not henceforth yield unto thee her strength; a fugitive and a vagabond shalt thou be in the earth. **13** And Cain said unto the Lord, My punishment *is* greater than I can bear. **14** Behold, thou hast driven me out this day from the face of the earth; and from thy face shall I be hid; and I shall be a fugitive and a vagabond in the earth; and it shall come to pass, *that* every one that findeth me shall slay me. **15** And the Lord said unto him, Therefore whosoever slayeth Cain, vengeance shall be taken on him sevenfold. And the Lord set a mark upon Cain, lest any finding him should kill him. **16** And Cain went out from the presence of the Lord, and dwelt in the land of Nod, on the east of Eden. **17** And Cain knew his wife; and she conceived, and bare Enoch: and he builded a city, and called the name of the city, after the name of his son, Enoch. **18** And unto Enoch was born Irad: and Irad begat Mehujael: and Mehujael begat Methusael: and Methusael begat Lamech. **19** And Lamech took unto him two wives: the name of the one *was* Adah, and the name of the other Zillah. **20** And Adah bare Jabal: he was the father of such as dwell in tents, and *of such as have* cattle. **21** And his brother's name *was* Jubal: he was the father of all such as handle the harp and organ. **22** And Zillah, she also bare Tubalcain, an instructer of every artificer in brass and iron: and the sister of Tubalcain *was* Naamah. **23** And Lamech said unto his wives, Adah and Zillah, Hear my voice; ye wives of Lamech, hearken unto my speech: for I have slain a man to my wounding, and a young man to my hurt. **24** If Cain shall be avenged sevenfold, truly Lamech seventy and sevenfold. **25** And Adam knew his wife again; and she bare a son, and called his name Seth: For God, *said she*, hath appointed me another seed instead of

Abel, whom Cain slew. **26** And to Seth, to him also there was born a son; and he called his name Enos: then began men to call upon the name of the Lord. **5:1a** This *is* the book of the generations of Adam.

*See the topic "Who Wrote Genesis" (pages 27-28) and the "Underline" activity below for information about the authorship of this section of Genesis.*

*Also see the photograph on p.70. It shows the splendid design and layout of the great east window of York Minster in York, England. One of the finest stained-glass treasures anywhere, from the Middle Ages. The top row shows scenes from the creation of the world and the fall of man into sin. See pages 66 and 67 for details of the creation panels.*

# Scripture Study

**Read.** You can read a book written by the first man, Adam. Yes, the first man could write. We know this was written, because it is called a *book* in its closing line. Also, it does not have the poetry form and mythological sound of an oral history. Instead, it has precise details, as an eyewitness might tell.

Adam and Eve were eyewitness to these events. They were the only people in the world to know the paradise garden with its Tree of Life and the Tree of Knowing Good and Evil. They were the only ones who knew what life was like without sin. They, alone, walked with God and talked face to face with Him. What do you suppose God told Adam during those walks?

Adam certainly had a lot to tell his descendants who never walked and talked with God. The Jews have a tradition that Adam wrote a long book about God, but it has been lost and we only have this short portion. But these few words tell us a lot about the beginnings of life in the world.

We have the great privilege of reading this ancient book written by the first man who ever lived.

**Underline** the names that Adam used for God. They are *Lord* or *Lord God* (which are *Jehovah* or *Jehovah Elohim* in Hebrew). Adam said "Lord" when he spoke of his Creator. But the serpent would not call Him "Lord." He only said, "God."

In God's book of creation, we don't find the name Jehovah. That came into use only with Adam's book.

**Draw** a map of Eden, the garden, and the surrounding lands, using information from 2:8-14. Your map may not look like someone else's map, because we can't tell from the description exactly where the lands are and where the rivers run. But your task is to draw a map that fits the information given. Your map will show that this geography is not found in the world today; Noah's Flood destroyed it all.

Note: One scholar spent ten years trying to match Eden's rivers with today's Tigris and Euphrates, or with buried rivers, the Nile and others. He did not succeed.

**List** Adam's descendents through Cain, which are named in chapter 4. Your list will begin with Adam and Eve and end with the three sons (and daughter) of Lamech, who are the eighth generation. The only woman descendant listed is Naamah. Some ancient Jews believed she is named because she became the wife of Noah.

**Memorize** 3:15. This is the first prophecy in the Bible. It tells who will be enemies until the end of the world. On one side of the war are the serpent Satan and his followers. On the other side are those of Eve's descendants, especially Christ, who belong to God. Satan will bruise the heel of Christ, this verse says, but Christ will win by crushing the head of Satan. The prophecy was fulfilled when Christ was bruised on the cross, but that same cross is what crushed Satan.

Satan's war began early in the world. And it will continue until the final battle described in Revelation 20.

# Topic Study

## Who Wrote Genesis?

We can tell who wrote different parts of Genesis because each part closes with a signature sentence. For instance, Adam's book closes with, "This is the book of the generations of Adam" (5:1). And Noah's book closes with, "These are the generations of Noah" (6:9a).

In this manner, the parts continue throughout Genesis. Adam and Noah were eyewitnesses to the events in their books, and the same is true of all other writers of Genesis. Adam's book tells about the garden of Eden, and of course he and his wife were the only people who saw and heard and experienced those events. Adam could write about other early events, too. He and Seth and others probably carefully kept the list of descendants and passed them down from father to son until the records reached Moses.

What about Moses, you may ask. Didn't he write Genesis? Genesis is one of the five "Books of Moses," but the Bible never says that Moses actually wrote it. The New Testament refers 25 times to specific things that Moses wrote in Exodus, Leviticus, Numbers and Deuteronomy. But it refers to Genesis over 200 times without ever saying that those are the words of Moses. (see *The Genesis Record* by Henry Morris, p. 29)

Genesis was not passed down as oral history, according to the evidence; it had to be written. One evidence is that it is not in poem form as oral traditions are. (Some examples of oral traditions are given later in this book.) Another evidence is the fact that the sun and moon are not named in God's book; they are just called lights. In later parts of Genesis they become the sun and moon, but never do they have names such as all early peoples gave them. Oral history tends to change over time because the storytellers use the names and language of their own times instead of retaining the original language.

Still another evidence from language is that the books written before Abram contain roots of words that were used in Sumer, but the books written after Abram moved to Canaan and visited Egypt contain words from Canaan and early Egypt. If Moses had written Genesis, all the style would have been from later Egypt.

Something we can see even in our English translations is evidence that Moses retained the original information but at times updated it with short editorial additions. For instance, 14:2 and 8 say "Bela, which is Zoar." Bela (BE luh) was the city's name in Isaac's time but Zoar (ZOE ar) was the name in Moses's time. So Moses retained the original history as Isaac wrote it but he identified the city for the people of his time. There are ten place names in Genesis which Moses updated in this way. When you read Genesis thoughtfully, you can find a few other editorial comments besides the place names. Perhaps Moses added the closing signatures which identify the writers of the sections.

So, it appears that Moses had the ancient books to work from. He compiled them, and in a few places added his editorial comments.

What is the closing sentence of the book of Adam?

When it says, "This is the book," does that make you think it is written history or oral history?

Tell one or more other sentences in Genesis that are similar to Adam's closing sentence.

Tell at least one language evidence that the books in Genesis were written earlier than Moses's time.

If someone says, "I think God revealed to Moses the past history, and Moses wrote all the words of Genesis," what argument (or arguments) could you give for the view that Adam and other early men wrote the history?

## The Strange Rivers of Eden (2:6,10-14)

We think it strange when we read that a river flowed from Eden to water the garden and then parted into four rivers. Rivers in our world do just the opposite. They flow into one another until four rivers might become one large river.

This gives us a clue that Adam's world was not like ours. Another clue is 2:6 which says that a mist watered the whole ground. Our ground gets watered mostly by rain.

Dr. Henry Morris, a hydrologist, who studies water, thinks the early earth had more underground water than now. The water bubbled up in springs which became the source of rivers. Over gentle landscape, the rivers would sometimes part, as in Eden, forming smaller rivers. Eventually the water would find its way underground again and the cycle could continue.

On cool mornings water vapor in the air would condense into droplets and form dew to water all the ground. No dark rain clouds moved in from large oceans. The geography of both water and land differed from today's earth.

Someday God will make the earth new again, and then we will see a river flowing out from the throne of God (Revelation 22:1). Will we also see it part into four rivers and flow to water the whole earth? We might. In many ways the new earth will be like the paradise Adam had before his world was cursed with sin.

This painting shows a statue of King Gudea of Sumer about 2270 B.C. His jar dispenses four streams of never-failing water of life. Other kings and gods in ancient times were shown in a similar pose, suggesting "rivers of living water" flowing from the belly (John 7:38). In some ancient sculptures the streams are watering the tree of life.

How was Eden's river different from today's rivers?

How were the crops watered in those days before the Flood when there was no rain?

In what way are the first river and the last river in the Bible alike?

# The Tree of Life

God planted the tree of life in the middle of Adam's garden. After Adam and Eve were put out of the garden, Cherubims (CHAIR yoo bimz) guarded so no one could get to the tree.

We never again see the tree of life until the last chapter of the Bible (Revelation 22:2). There in the holy city we see it growing beside the river which flows clear as crystal from the throne of God.

Adam and Eve saw the tree of life at the beginning of time in Eden, and all the redeemed shall see it at the end of time in the holy Jerusalem. A painting from the Middle Ages shows God seated on the throne, with the Lamb at His right hand. The river flows from the throne, and the tree of life grows on both its banks. An angel shows the vision to John. From a hand-illustrated manuscript, *Apocalypse*, of the 1200s. (See painting on page 68)

The long history of the tree of life in art. LEFT ABOVE: From a cylinder seal in ancient, pagan Assyria. The tree is guarded by two griffins, with head and wings of an eagle and body of a lion. These creatures are likely a pagan version of Cherubims. RIGHT ABOVE: Many centuries later (A.D. 1026) in Italy, almost the same pattern is seen in a window of a Christian church. LEFT BELOW: A stylized version of the tree found in ancient Mesopotamia and used, with variations, in many areas for thousands of years. RIGHT BELOW: Ramses II on the throne of Egypt, while gods write his name on the fruits of the tree of life.

The tree of life stylized in a border design from ancient Assyria.

**Praise for the Tree of Life**

Jesus, thy glory fills the skies,
  Plant of renown thou art,
A tree desired to make one wise
  And cheer a drooping heart.

Upon this fruit whoever feeds
  No want nor care he knows.
No other fruit he seeks nor needs;
  This healeth all his woes.

*(From a tract by R. Peach, printed in Birmingham, England, about 1770.)*

ABOVE: Persian carpets contain many variations of the tree of life, even up to the present time. RIGHT: Pagodas also show a tree form, because Buddhists believe enlightenment came from the cosmic tree, or tree of life.

Border design from Greece, many centuries later than the border at left.

Artists all through history have made the tree of life one of their most common themes. In some drawings four rivers pour down from the tree in essentially the same direction. In others four rivers radiate from the tree toward the four directions of the compass. The rivers and the tree were known all over the world, even where people didn't have the Bible.

In pagan art and mythology the tree is the very center of the world, its roots reaching down to the underworld and its branches leading up to heaven. It is sometimes called the cosmic tree or the world tree. Heroes and gods are said to have descended to the underworld and ascended to heaven by the tree. Buddha is said to have attained enlightenment under such a tree. Pagodas are built from the shape of the tree. Wall paintings of the tree in Egyptian tombs were believed to give eternal life to the dead. Persian carpets and Islamic prayer carpets have tree-of-life motifs woven into them.

Sometimes a serpent is drawn with the tree, and we know where that idea came from. Sometimes two bulls or mythical animals are shown on either side of the tree. Such drawings have been dug up from Sumer, the earliest civilization we know. Those drawings were made not long after Noah's Flood and thus are the oldest art known to history.

The god Hermes was said to carry a rod, symbol of the tree, entwined with serpents. Later, a Greek physician used this rod as a symbol for healing, and it is still used as the emblem of physicians today.

The fact that the tree of life was so widely known all over the world is evidence that the original tree of life was real. Only in Adam's book do we have the pure story as written by the one man in history who, with his wife, saw the original tree. The Apostle John later saw the tree in the new Jerusalem.

A physicians' emblem as it may be seen today.

We believers will see it too, someday. It will yield twelve fruits, fruit for every month; and its leaves will heal the nations.

You can read about the tree of life in which two books of the Bible?

Why do you think a serpent is often shown with the tree in ancient art? Does the serpent help you identify which tree it is?

Why are rivers sometimes shown with the tree in ancient art? Do the rivers help you identify which tree it is?

Describe the symbol of the medical profession.

# The Border Sacrifice

Where did Adam make his offerings to God and teach his sons how to do it? Many Bible scholars believe they sacrificed at the east gate of the garden, under the Cherubims who were keeping the way of the tree of life. Elsewhere in Old Testament times people met the Lord of life under cherubims.

For instance, in the times of the tabernacle, God commanded His people to make two gold cherubims and to set them over the mercy seat, which was over the ark of the covenant. God said He would speak with Moses from between those cherubims. The gold cherubims were no doubt patterned after the real Cherubims from heaven.

Adam saw those real Cherubims. The King James translators used a capital C to write about them. All other cherubims in the Bible are golden

Four-winged cherubims as they may have appeared on the ark of the covenant.

images or are visions, and they are not capitalized. Here are some of the Bible passages which show that God dwelt between the cherubims and spoke with men from there.

- God told Moses to make golden cherubims for the tabernacle (Exodus 25:18-22).

- God spoke to Moses from between the gold cherubims (Numbers 7:89).

- David moved the ark, which was "called by the name of the Lord of hosts that dwellest between the cherubims" (II Samuel 6:2).

- The ark was put under the cherubims in Solomon's new temple, and the glory of the Lord "filled the house of the Lord" (I Kings 8:6-11).

- Hezekiah and some of the psalmists prayed to the God which dwelt "between the cherubims" (II Kings 19:15; Psalms 80:1 and 99:1).

- Ezekiel saw a heavenly vision of the cherubims and the glory of the Lord above them (Ezekiel 10:1-22).

Besides Bible evidence, we have historical and linguistic evidence that Adam worshipped God under the Cherubims at the border of the garden. Two samples of ancient Chinese characters are shown here. In the first, you can see the garden of Eden divided by four rivers. Beside it are three graceful lines which stand for Shangti, the Creator God. The bent line at right is a person bowing before God. Used together, these lines form a character for border. An older meaning for this character is "to come before God." (Shangti is similar to a Hebrew name for God, El Shaddai.)

border

In the second character, two persons bow beside the garden. Two are indicated by the two lines beside the bent person. Could

border

the two have come from Cain and Abel? Or from Adam and Seth? Together, these lines form another character which means border. So it looks as if the ancient Chinese, in writing *border* or *come before God*, fashioned their symbols after the first important border known to history.

For over 4000 years Chinese emperors traveled each year to the border of the country or the border of the capital city to make a sacrifice. This annual ceremony began before the first emperors known to history, more than 2000 years before Christ. And it continued until 1911 when the Manchu emperors were deposed.

Confucius (con FEW shus) wrote of these border sacrifices but he did not know their meaning. It was a puzzle, he said. Sadly, the Chinese had lost the stories of the early world, even though their ancestors put many of them into the writing system. (This information from *Mysteries Consucius Couldn't Solve* by Ethel R. Nelson and Richard E Broadberry.)

Where were the real Cherubims that Adam saw?

Where were the golden cherubims in the time of Moses? In the time of Solomon?

Was God's presence associated with the gold cherubims? With the cherubims in Exekiel's vision?

Do you think God met Adam by the real Cherubims? Why, or why not?

What do you think was the origin of the Chinese long custom of offering a border sacrifice?

# The Curses (3:14-19)

After Adam and Eve sinned, God spoke some curses. He cursed the serpent, He pronounced sorrow and death for the man and his wife, and He cursed the earth itself.

These curses are still working. We believers understand very well that we are sinners like Adam and Eve, and that we need the salvation that God provides through Jesus Christ. This gives us a good understanding of the condition of mankind—what we are like, where we came from, what our purpose is on earth, and what our destiny is. The world's psychologists and philosophers don't know as much as we do about the age-old question, "What is man?"

Do we understand the curse on the earth as well as the curses on people? Perhaps not. Perhaps we have heard too much of evolutionary ideas. We may forget that the curse brought weeds, disease, decay and death to the world. The world is running down. It is wearing out. It can't last forever.

That is not bad news. It is good news. God said the curse was for Adam's sake (3:17), and that means for our sake also. It is better to die to the world and get new life through Christ. In the end we will get a new world, too (Revelation 21:1).

The last chapter of the Bible says "there shall be no more curse" (Revelation 22:3).

When did death first come to the world? Why did it come?

If there was no death before Adam's sin, does this tell you that the dinosaurs died before Adam or after Adam? (More on dinosaurs later.)

Do you think Adam could have dug up any fossils? Explain.

John wrote the book of Revelation. Did John know about the curse of Genesis?

## The End of the Curse

Do you like to peek at the last page of a book to see how the story ends? You can do that with the earth's story.

The story of our world began with God creating it good, and then very soon Adam sinned and God cursed the earth. Here are some conditions in our world now because of the curse.

> ground is cursed
> thorns grow
> people have sorrow
> people have pain and sickness
> people die
> earth is wearing out
> the Tree of Life is unavailable
> Satan is our enemy

The end of the story is told in the last two chapters of Revelation, where God makes a new heaven and new earth (21:1). Here is a partial list of what we find there.

> no more curse (22:3)
> no sorrow, pain or death (21:4)
> God makes a new earth (21:1)
> eat from the Tree of Life (22:14)
> Satan cast out forever (20:10)

What a wonderful ending! Will you be there?

Name three or more results of the curse on the earth.

Name three or more ways the new earth will be different from this cursed earth.

# Where Did Cain Get His Wife?

When you talk to people about Genesis, a common question they ask is, "Where did Cain get his wife?" If they don't believe Genesis, they're really trying to say, "See? People evolved in several places, because Cain found a wife over in Nod." (A more thorough treatment of this question is found in *The Answer Book* by Ham et al.)

You can be ready to answer this question. It's easy. The story in the Bible says nothing about where Cain found his wife. It just says that Cain fled to Nod, and he and his wife began to have children. So we can fill in the missing details in a way that fits the Bible story better.

Adam and Eve had many children (5:4). At first, brothers and sisters married each other, which was okay in those early days while the gene pool was so new and healthy. Later, people married cousins and nieces for a while. There were a lot of people by the time Cain fled to Nod. In fact, people were the reason Cain had to flee, as he complained to God. "Every one that findeth me shall slay me" (4:14). So God put a mark upon Cain so that people wanting vengeance would not kill him. Then Cain took his wife to Nod with him, and they began to have children there.

So when someone asks, "Where did Cain get his wife?" you can show him that there really is no problem with the Bible story.

Does the Bible account say that Cain went to Nod and found a wife among some people there?

Does the Bible account say that Cain took his wife to Nod?

Does the Bible account omit the detail about where Cain got his wife?

Do you think it makes more sense to say Cain found his wife in Nod or to say he took his wife to Nod? Why?

## Basic World Views

The first man in the world has a lot to tell us about ourselves. His book is packed with information about our beginnings as the race of mankind. From this true information, we can shape our world views. And when we live by correct world views we live happier lives. Here are some major truths about mankind found in Adam's book.

**Mankind was created by God** and received life from Him. This is a high view of man compared with the evolutionary view that life arose spontaneously and we are descended from animals. This high view makes us answerable to God our Creator.

**People have a sinful nature.** When Adam sinned, he fell from his original righteous state to a sinful state. And sin leads to death. Elsewhere in the

Bible we read that we all inherit Adam's sin and death. One example: "Wherefore, as by one man sin entered into the world, and death by sin; and so death passed upon all men. (Romans 5:12).

**God provides the remedy for our sin.** This remedy was first announced to Adam in the garden, and it unfolds throughout the rest of the Bible. Paul explained it simply: "For as in Adam all die, even so in Christ shall all be made alive" (I Corinthians 15:22).

**God instituted the family** before any other human institution. God's family plan consists of one husband and one wife leaving their parents and becoming one, with the husband ruling over his wife. Children are to be nurtured in such families and this provides the foundation of all else in society.

**People need work.** Even before Adam sinned, God gave him the work of tilling the ground and having dominion over the earth and the creatures in it. God ordained work from the beginning.

> Try to explain some differences between the creationist view and the evolutionist view of how mankind began.

> If you believe that God made you, will you live differently from someone who believes that humans happened by chance to come from animals? What might some of these differences be?

> All of us are sinners. What was the original cause of that?

> The first announcement of God's remedy for sin is in the memory verse, 3:15. Can you explain the part about bruising the head?

> What did God start first—church or nation or school or family? Do you think God knows best how we should live?

> Do you think you and your family would be happy without any work to do? Try to back up your answer with something from Adam's book.

# Myths of Man's Origin

All myths of the origin of mankind fall into two categories. One category is where the gods make people. They form people from earth and water or stones or something, or they give birth to people in various ways and then take away their immortality. The second category is where people just develop out of earth or water with no help from gods.

No other category is possible, in ancient times or now. We can believe either that a divine spirit is eternal and created everything or that matter is eternal and exists by its own power. Which came first, spirit or matter?

Here is a Greek myth of the first category, showing the gods making a human. It contains remnants of Adam's original story of Eve.

---

### Pandora

Zeus told one of the gods to mix earth and water to form a woman. So the god made a beautiful maiden from the clay and she was named Pandora. Then Zeus told the other gods to each bring a gift of one of his own attributes. All these gifts were harmful except for one. Zeus put them into a box, presented it to Pandora, and forbade her ever to open the box. Then he sent her to Epimetheus, who gladly accepted this first woman in the world.

Pandora was very curious, and one day she opened the lid for just a peek. Suddenly out flew sickness and sorrows and death and evils of all kinds. She slammed the lid shut, but it was too late. There was no capturing the evils now. They were loose in the world.

Only one gift remained after she shut the lid. Hope. That is all mankind has now to comfort him in the midst of the evils.

---

Here is a myth with the opposite view—that there were no gods. It couldn't have its beginning in Adam's story. Could it have begun from a false story that Satan started? Satan's first view of the world may have been when it was formless water, before God called out the land and other forms.

This story sounds strangely like modern evolutionism.

---

### From Phoenicia

In the beginning, all was dark and windy, and the winds twisted themselves into Desire. Desire made a watery slime called Mot. From Mot came simple living creatures that had no consciousness. From the simple creatures came more complex creatures until at last some were conscious.

The conscious beings could think about the heavens, the sun, moon, stars and planets. They looked below and saw that Mot was egg-shaped and shining.

---

From the myths are descended the folktales, and we can discover bits of original truth in them, also. For instance, an Uncle Remus story from Africa tells of Brer Rabbit getting more and more stuck in the Tar Baby trap. At first he only looked, then he touched and then he was caught, similar to Eve and the fruit. Cinderella and many other tales look back to the original hero of Genesis 3:15, where all the world should look for its redemption.

From the Pandora myth, what remnants can you find of the
  Bible's true story of Eve?

Can you describe the two types of belief found among
  ancient peoples about the origin of humans?

Would you say those two beliefs still exist today?

Would you call evolutionary beliefs the mythology of our
  own times? What do you think people 1000 years from
  now will call it?

Thinking of folktales that you know, can you detect any
  remnant of original truth in them?

## Heroes and Dragon Slaying

Hero stories have run through all the world's literature from early days
until now. We meet the prototype of all heroes as early as the garden of Eden
(3:15). The hero will slay the serpent at great cost to himself.

You can meet descendants of this hero in ancient myths where he strug-
gles with fierce evils and wins. He may journey through dangers and trials to
gain the golden fleece or golden apples. You can meet later descendants of
the hero in folktales and "fairy tales" (which seldom are about fairies). You
can recognize this hero in many ways. He may be the king's son. He may be
hidden as a baby because the pretender to the throne wants to kill him. He
may be sent on a dangerous journey to earn the right to rule, even though the
right was his all the time. Through his bravery he may win the beautiful bride.
Many literature teachers say that Christ is the original hero from which all
those heroes come.

The serpent or dragon in all ancient stories represents evil, and the hero
represents good. This symbolism lived for thousands of years, right down
to modern times. But, unfortunately, in our times the dragon is sometimes
portrayed as a benign, friendly creature. He is loved by children. They sing
cheery songs about him. This violates the biblical world view that should
shape our literature and art as well as every other field. (More on dragons in
the Dinosaur topic of Unit IV. Also in the Dragon topic of Unit I.)

What common theme runs through literature from ancient
  times until now?

What do some literature professors say is the source of the
  hero theme?

What does the serpent symbolize in most of the world's
  literature? How have recent writers and artists violated
  that long tradition?

# *Further Study*

**1. Correlated Readings.** Below are two suggested readings which correlate with Adam's book. The first is easier, narrative reading, and the second is advanced verse-by-verse study.

a) *Adam and His Kin by Ruth Beechick, chapters 2 to 6.*
b) *The Genesis Record by Henry Morris, pages 22 to 30 and 82 to 151.*

**2. Book Signatures.** An easy way to explain to friends about the authors of Genesis is to have the signatures marked in your Bible. Each mark leads to the next, so all you have to remember is to start at 2:4.

To prepare, underline the signature in 2:4 and beside it write 5:1. Turn to 5:1, underline the signature and beside it write the next reference, and so forth. Here are the signatures for the first six books.

| | |
|---|---|
| **2:4** | These are the generations of the heavens and of the earth when they were created. |
| **5:1** | This is the book of the generations of Adam. |
| **6:9** | These are the generations of Noah. |
| **10:1** | Now these are the generations of the sons of Noah. |
| **11:10** | These are the generations of Shem. |
| **11:27** | Now these are the generations of Terah. |

Perhaps you noticed that the first words of each book often repeat information that ended the previous book. There's a good reason for this. It's because if you were reading from the original stone tablets, that's how you would tell which one follows which. Archeologists find that kind of pattern on many ancient tablets.

Signatures for the rest of Genesis are given below in case you want to mark them, also, in your Bible. These latter books are more complicated to follow than the first six because some short books are embedded within longer books. The three long books are one by Abram and Isaac, one by Jacob, and the last by the sons of Jacob (Israel).

The last signature has a slightly different pattern than the others, but if we change the word names to generations, we see that it really is similar. This last book is filled with information that could only have been written by Joseph and his brothers. It contains details about Egyptian people and practices that could be known only by someone in Joseph's generation and not by someone writing in Moses's time or later. Its style indicates that it was written in Egypt, whereas earlier books were written in Mesopotamia, where Terah lived, and where Abram lived the first part of his life.

**25:12** Now these are the generations of Ishmael. (This introduces a short book which is embedded near the end of the book listed below.)

**25:19**   And these are the generations of Isaac, Abraham's son. (This
signature ends the book of records which Abraham began and
Isaac completed. Ishmael's short book listed above probably
was attached to this at the time Isaac and Ishmael buried their
father Abraham.)

**36:1 and 36:9** . . . these are the generations of Esau. (These signatures
introduce Esau's records, which take up all of chapter 36.
They are embedded within the book listed below.)

**37:2**   These are the generations of Jacob.

**Exodus 1:1**   Now these are the names of the children of Israel
[Jacob].

**3. Other Readings.** Below are reading suggestions from the Bible and
from old tales that follow up some of the many themes introduced in Adam's
book.

*a)   Revelation.* The end of the world's story is in Revelation 21 and 22.
Read this yourself or with your family. Compare with our present cursed earth
and see if you can add to the list given in the section on "The End of the
Curse."

The end of the dragon is found in Revelation 20:1-3,10.

*b)   Old Tales.* Old tales are sometimes called "fairy tales" or "folktales."
Many of these are descended from ancient mythology, which in turn are descended from original true stories from the books of God, Adam and Noah or
from Satan's false version of how the world began and what early people did.

If your family wants to read some of these stories, you can try to recognize remnants of the originals.

**4. Writing.** Write a sentence about each of these four topics that clearly
explains to someone what you believe about it:

*1)* the beginning of mankind;
*2)* our fall into sin;
*3)* the curse that sin caused;
*4)* how all this will end.

Next, form your sentences into a paragraph with a bit of editing if necessary, and see how you have explained what your world view is.

You may expand this into an essay if you like, by writing a paragraph or
more on each of the four points listed.

*Below: Tree of Life border design from ancient Rome.*

# Unit III

## *Book of Noah*

*"And God said unto Noah . . . Make thee an ark of gopher wood" (from Genesis 6:1 3, 1 4). Building Noah's Ark, a painting in one of the most beautiful handmade books of the Middle Ages, called* The Bedford Hours, *and made for the Duke of Bedford and his French wife, Anne, in 1423. Several artists worked on the book and their names are unknown. This artist shows a pre-Flood world of herders and castles and sailing ships with God and two angels looking down upon it all.*

# Scripture Text

## Book of Noah

**Genesis 5:1b** In the day that God created man, in the likeness of God made he him; **2** Male and female created he them; and blessed them, and called their name Adam, in the day when they were created. **3** And Adam lived an hundred and thirty years, and begat *a son* in his own likeness, and after his image; and called his name Seth: **4** And the days of Adam after he had begotten Seth were eight hundred years: and he begat sons and daughters: **5** And all the days that Adam lived were nine hundred and thirty years: and he died. **6** And Seth lived an hundred and five years, and begat Enos: **7** And Seth lived after he begat Enos eight hundred and seven years, and begat sons and daughters: **8** And all the days of Seth were nine hundred and twelve years: and he died. **9** And Enos lived ninety years, and begat Cainan: **10** And Enos lived after he begat Cainan eight hundred and fifteen years, and begat sons and daughters: **11** And all the days of Enos were nine hundred and five years: and he died. **12** And Cainan lived seventy years and begat Mahalaleel: **13** And Cainan lived after he begat Mahalaleel eight hundred and forty years, and begat sons and daughters: **14** And all the days of Cainan were nine hundred and ten years: and he died. **15** And Mahalaleel lived sixty and five years, and begat Jared: **16** And Mahalaleel lived after he begat Jared eight hundred and thirty years, and begat sons and daughters: **17** And all the days of Mahalaleel were eight hundred ninety and five years: and he died. **18** And Jared lived an hundred sixty and two years, and he begat Enoch: **19** And Jared lived after he begat Enoch eight hundred years, and begat sons and daughters: **20** And all the days of Jared were nine hundred sixty and two years: and he died. **21** And Enoch lived sixty and five years, and begat Methuselah: **22** And Enoch walked with God after he begat Methuselah three hundred years, and begat sons and daughters: **23** And all the days of Enoch were three hundred sixty and five years: **24** And Enoch walked with God: and he *was* not; for God took him. **25** And Methuselah lived an hundred eighty and seven years, and begat Lamech. **26** And Methuselah lived after he begat Lamech seven hundred eighty and two years, and begat sons and daughters: **27** And all the days of Methuselah were nine hundred sixty and nine years: and he died. **28** And Lamech lived an hundred eighty and two years, and begat a son: **29** And he called his name Noah, saying, This *same* shall comfort us concerning our work and toil of our hands, because of the ground which the Lord hath cursed. **30** And Lamech lived after he begat Noah five hundred ninety and five years, and begat sons and daughters: **31** And all the days of Lamech were seven hundred seventy and seven years: and he died. **32** And Noah was five hundred years old: and Noah begat Shem, Ham, and Japheth.

**Genesis 6:1**  And it came to pass, when men began to multiply on the face of the earth, and daughters were born unto them, **2** That the sons of God saw the daughters of men that they *were* fair; and they took them wives of all which they chose. **3** And the Lord said, My spirit shall not always strive with man, for that he also *is* flesh: yet his days shall be an hundred and twenty years. **4** There were giants in the earth in those days; and also after that, when the sons of God came in unto the daughters of men, and they bare *children* to them, the same *became* mighty men which *were* of old, men of renown. **5** And God saw that the wickedness of man *was* great in the earth, and *that* every imagination of the thoughts of his heart *was* only evil continually. **6** And it repented the Lord that he had made man on the earth, and it grieved him at his heart. **7** And the Lord said, I will destroy man whom I have created from the face of the earth; both man, and beast, and the creeping thing, and the fowls of the air; for it repenteth me that I have made them. **8** But Noah found grace in the eyes of the Lord. **9** These *are* the generations of Noah: . . .

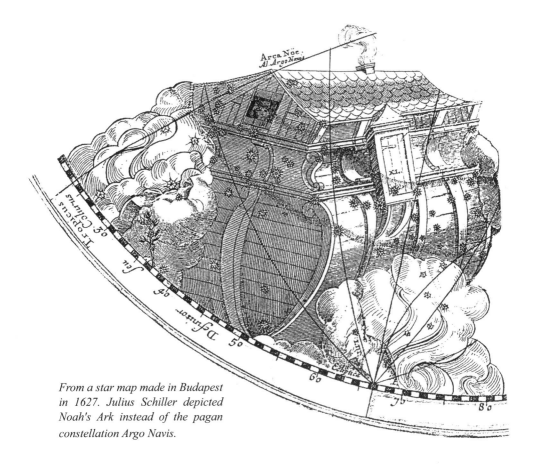

*From a star map made in Budapest in 1627. Julius Schiller depicted Noah's Ark instead of the pagan constellation Argo Navis.*

# Scripture Study

**Read** this short book by the great man Noah. The first part gives a family tree, which must have been passed down from Seth and others until it reached Noah. The last part tells a little about how wicked the world was before God sent the Flood. Noah may have written more, but Moses included this part in his book of beginnings.

**Mark** numerals 1, 2, 3 and so forth beside the name of each man in the generations from Adam to Noah. You should find 10 in all.

**List** all the patriarchs from Adam to Noah. These follow the line of Seth, but some names are similar to names in the line of Seth's brother Cain. After each man's name, write his age when his named son was born and write his age at death. Save this list to use if you make the graph suggested for the book of Terah.

For Noah's death, look ahead at verse 9:29. Noah's eldest son was Japheth (10:21), but Shem is the son you'll need on this list. In the arithmetic project later, there is help for finding Shem's birth date.

**Compare** your list (above) with the list in I Chronicles 1:1-4. Both those lists were in the Bible that Jesus used and believed and quoted. Luke wrote the genealogy again. Compare your list with Luke 3:36c-38.

**Memorize** 6:8. In this closing statement of his book, Noah did not claim to be righteous. God called him righteous (Ezekiel 14:14). Peter called him a preacher of righteousness (II Peter 2:5). And Noah's sons called him a just man and perfect (6:9b). But Noah said only that he found grace in God's eyes.

# Topic Study

## Giants in the Earth

Were giants real in history? Yes, they were. Here's what Noah's book says about giants.

> "There were giants in the earth in those days; and also after that, when the sons of God came in unto the daughters of men, and they bare children to them, the same became mighty men which were of old, men of renown" (6:4).

Who were those sons of God who became fathers of giants? In Scripture, "sons of God" refers to creatures directly created by God.

The very first sons were angels who shouted for joy when God laid the foundations of the earth (Job 38:7). After some angels fell, they were still called sons of God (Job 2:1). We sometimes call them demons or evil spirits. Those evil creatures are who Noah wrote about in the verse quoted above. The Greek Bible that Jesus used actually calls them angels in this verse instead of sons of God. (This Greek translation of the Hebrew Scriptures is called the Septuagint.) This was Satan's plan to corrupt the whole human race so Jesus could not be born from the seed of the woman and become our Savior.

That first prophecy given in Eden (Genesis 3:15) was coming to pass. Satan's seed and Eve's seed were enemies at war.

God saw the terrible wickedness and found only Noah "perfect in his generations." So He planned to destroy the world and save only Noah's pure line so Jesus could be born later in history.

If you read verse 6:4 carefully, you can detect where an editor must have added some phrases to Noah's record. Probably Moses wrote, "in those days; and also after that." He refers to the days of Noah and to a later time when some giants lived in the land of Canaan after the Flood. Other nations, too, including England, have traditions of giants living in their lands in the early days. (See pages 78-79 for information about giants in England.)

Moses probably also added the words, "the same became mighty men which were of old, men of renown." It seems that already in Moses's time there were stories about men known for mighty acts of strength, and about beings who were half god and half human. Later the Greeks had similar stories. In fact, all over the world are stories, which we call myths, which no doubt began in those early times.

The Bible gives only this little information about evil in the world, and then proceeds with the wonderful story of how God saved Noah and his family on the ark.

Here's more we should know about the Bible term "sons of God." Adam was called a son of God because he was directly created by God (Luke 3:38). After we are saved, we become newly created sons of God (John 1:12).

What is the meaning of "son of God"?

Why are angels called sons of God?

Why is Adam called a son of God?

When can you be called a son (or daughter) of God?

Where do you think the Greek and Roman tales of giants and gods got their start?

If demons (fallen angels) contact humans today in UFOs as aliens, or in any form, what should Christians do? (Answer: Don't get curious, stay far away, have nothing to do with these activities.)

# Biographies

Most of Noah's book is genealogy (je ne AH lo je), a list of ancestors in his family tree. Noah's list is repeated at the opening of I Chronicles. The historian Luke wrote the list again in his book, at the end of Luke 3.

There are ten generations. Only eight of these men were rulers, or head preachers, because Enoch went to heaven while his father still lived, and Lamech died while his father still lived. Thus these two never became head priests or preachers. That made Noah the eighth, a preacher of righteousness (II Peter 2:5). One king list dug up in ancient Sumer names eight kings before the Flood and another names ten kings. (More about these kings in the book of Terah.)

Following is information on some of the ancestors that Noah listed.

**Adam.** God breathed life into Adam's body and Adam became a living person who could think and talk with God right from the beginning. Old Jewish tradition says that Adam and Eve lived in the garden of Eden for seven years before they sinned and had to leave the garden. The Bible does not tell us how long it was.

After the garden years, Cain and Abel were born, and later, Seth. Adam also had other children who are not named in the Bible (5:4). According to tradition, the number was 33 sons and 23 daughters. Tradition means history which is passed down through many generations, which might be true or partly true, but we can't be sure. It sounds possible for Adam to have that many children, since he lived more than 900 years.

Jewish tradition also says that Adam wrote a book about God. If that's true and if you lived before the Flood, you could have read about God from the man who walked and talked with Him in the garden before sin entered the world. Because people lived so long in those days, many generations could have heard Adam tell about God, even down to Noah's grandfather.

The name Adam means *man* or, as we might say today, *mankind*.

**Seth.** The meaning of Seth's name is *appointed*. The parents, Adam and Eve, thought either that this child was appointed to take the place of Abel, who was killed, or that he was appointed to bring salvation. They were partly right, because through Seth's line Christ came later in history. According to tradition Seth, along with his father Adam and his son Enoch, invented the science of astronomy. Seth and other pre-Flood preachers are said to have read in the skies of God's great glory and His plan to redeem the world. They could use the stars as visual aids to help people remember their sermons. (Pagans, though, so perverted the system of reading the skies that God judged them at Babel, and now we are supposed to read God's Word, not the skies.) Since the constellations were quite similar all over the ancient world, this shows that the system must have started from one place and spread outward. If different nations invented astronomy separately, the systems would have been different. So the constellation pictures we know today may have begun with Seth. (Did Seth perhaps invent the sky visual of the hero crushing the serpent? See the sky maps shown in Unit VI.)

**Enos.** In the days of Enos "men began to call upon the name of the Lord" (4:26 KJV). An ancient Jewish commentator, Maimonides, says that the word call could mean *profane* as in Leviticus 19:12. If this is the correct meaning, this sentence tells the sad story that the third generation, even in Seth's line, had already fallen from the true worship of God. Another suggestion for this word is that at this time God removed the Cherubim and no longer met with worshipers at the gate of the garden; thus mankind had to "call" upon God in a new way. With either of these interpretations, men would be impressed with their mortality. The name *Enos* means *mortal*.

**Enoch.** Enoch's name means *teaching*, and he did teach. We know from the Bible (Jude 14) as well as from tradition that Enoch (EE nok) was a prophet. Though Enoch's book or books are lost to us, we do have two ancient books named Enoch which were written much later in history by someone who used Enoch's name, and they include a few quotes from Enoch's original prophecies. Jude quotes one prophecy which tells that the Lord will return with ten thousands of His saints to execute judgment upon all the ungodly (Jude 14,15). Enoch never died. God took him up at 365 years of age, which was young in those days. The only other man who never died is Elijah, who went up in a chariot of fire. Will these be the two witnesses who return in the end times (Revelation 11:3-12)?

**Methuselah.** Methuselah (meh THOO zuh luh) lived for 969 years. People like to ask this riddle:

Methuselah was the oldest man who ever lived, yet he died before his father. How can that be?

The answer is that Enoch was his father, and Enoch didn't die.

The name Methuselah means, "In the year he dies, it shall come," and his father Enoch put that prophecy into the child's name. A shorter way to say it in English is: his death shall bring. Knowing that prophecy, people should have been getting ready for the judgment as Methuselah got older and older. Since Methuselah lived so long, it looks as if God waited and waited, to give people time to repent and turn from their wickedness. But at last Methuselah died and the Flood came that same year, just as predicted. His grandson Noah was ready with the ark.

**Lamech.** We know nothing about Lamech's (LAY mek) life, but his name means *despairing*. Does that characterize the age in which he lived? Did God's people despair because of great wickedness in the world? Lamech named his son Noah, which means *comfort* or *rest.* Gary Hedrick of the Christian Jew Foundation says the Hebrew language here indicates that Lamech thought Noah was to be the Messiah. God's people before the Flood despaired of wickedness but looked for God's salvation, just as we despair of the wickedness around us, but look for Jesus to come.

**Noah.** The stories of Noah and the ark are probably among the best known stories around the world. The Bible tells us, also, of one episode where Noah became drunk and later blessed and cursed his progeny. It is left for us to speculate on whether he had other children besides the three who were born after God first announced that He would destroy man from the face of the earth. Ancient Jewish tradition says that Noah did have children in his first 500 years, but they were lost with the rest of the wicked world.

Which patriarch did not die?

Which man is said to have invented astronomy?

Which man was Noah's grandfather?

What does the Bible say happened in the time of Enos?

Which man was Noah's father?

Which man died in the year of the Flood?

Were Cain, Abel, and Seth the only sons that Adam had?

Which man had the longest life span?

What does Lamech's name mean?

What does Noah's name mean?

# Hidden Message

Do you know what your name means? We all know what Joy means. Some Germans may remember that Howard means *brave heart*, and a few people may know that George means *farmer* in Greek.

People who know Hebrew have figured out the meanings of most Bible names, and you can find below the ten names from Adam to Noah. Look at these meanings and then read the surprise which follows them.

| | |
|---|---|
| Adam | Man |
| Seth | Appointed |
| Enosh | Mortal |
| Kenan | Sorrow |
| Mahalalel | The blessed God |

(Our paise word *hallelujah* can be seen in the name *Mahalalel.*)

| | |
|---|---|
| Jared | Shall come down |

| Enoch | Teaching |
| Methuselah | His death shall bring |
| Lamech | The despairing |
| Noah | Comfort, Rest |

Now connect the names to see what they say all together: Man [is] appointed mortal sorrow [but] the blessed God shall come down teaching [that] His death shall bring the despairing comfort, rest.

> The gospel message is that we are all sinners and God's Son died to bring us salvation. Do you think this gospel message is found in the Genesis message above? Explain.

## What Was Noah's Wife's Name?

Maybe we can know Mrs. Noah's name. It comes from southwest China, where Maio (MY oh) tribes tell their history orally. Oral histories are in verse form, because that helps the memory. The Maio have passed their history down for thousands of years, yet it contains numerous details that agree with the Bible accounts of creation, the Flood, and the high tower and the changing of languages. At weddings the Maio recite the ancestors of the bride and groom all the way back to Adam, so they practice quite often. A part of their history is given below. Patriarch Dirt is Adam, who was made from the dust of the earth. We can also easily recognize the names of Seth, Lamech, Noah and Noah's three sons. And we find a name for Mrs. Noah.

### *Maio Oral History*

Patriarch: (PAY tre ark) is the male head of a family or tribal line.

*The Patriarch Dirt begat Patriarch Se-teh.*
*The Patriarch Se-Teh begat a son Lusu.*
*And Lusu had Gehlo and he begat Lama.*
*The Patriarch Lama begat the man Nuah.*
*His wife was the Matriarch Gaw Bo-lu-en.*
*Their sons were Lo Han, Lo Shen and Jah-hu.*

Godhead: Divine nature; the character or quality of being God.

*So the earth began filling*
*With tribes and with families.*
*Creation was shared*
*By the clans and the peoples.*
*These did not God's will*
*Nor returned His affection,*
*But fought with each other*
*Defying the Godhead.*
*Their leaders shook fists*
*In the face of the Mighty.*

*Then the earth was convulsed*
*To the depth of three strata,*
*Rending the air*
*To the uttermost heaven.*
*God's anger arose*
*Till His Being was changed;*
*His wrath flaring up*
*Filled His eyes and His face*
*Until He must come*
*And demolish humanity—*
*Come and destroy*
*A whole world full of people.*

*So it poured forty days*
*In sheets and in torrents,*
*Then fifty-five days*
*Of misting and drizzle.*
*The waters surmounted*
*The mountains and ranges.*
*The deluge ascending*
*Leapt valley and hollow.*
*An earth with no earth*
*Upon which to take refuge!*
*A world with no foothold*
*Where one might subsist!*
*The people were baffled,*
*Impotent and ruined,*
*Despairing, horror stricken,*
*Diminished and finished.*
*But the Patriarch Nuah was righteous.*
*The Matriarch Gaw Bo-lu-en upright.*
*Built a boat very wide.*
*Made a ship very vast.*
*Their household entire*
*Got aboard and were floated,*
*The family complete*
*Rode the deluge in safety.*

From "Impact"
April 1991. Institute for Creation Research.

How many probable matches can you make between the Maio names and Bible names?

Find one or more events in the Maio history that are like Bible history.

Find one or more events in the Maio history that are not in
the Bible history.

What do you think accounts for these differences?

## New Testament Noah

Does the New Testament affirm that Noah and the Flood were a real part
of history? Yes. Jesus and Peter and the writer of Hebrews all mentioned Noah.

**Jesus** used the history of Noah's time as an example for teaching about
a future time. Jesus reminded His disciples that people ate and drank and
married right up until Noah entered the ark and the Flood came and destroyed
them all. He said that's the way it will be someday when Jesus returns; most
people will not be ready (Matthew 24:37-39; Luke 17:27).

**Peter** used the Noah history as Jesus did, to teach that God will spare the
righteous when judgment comes again. In the Flood God saved just Noah's
family (I Peter 3:20; II Peter 2:5).

**Paul**, or whoever wrote Hebrews, used Noah as a great example of
faith. Noah hadn't seen rain or a great cataclysm of water on the earth, but he
believed God anyway and built the ark (Hebrews 11:7).

Does Jesus believe the story of Noah and the Flood?

How do you know?

What New Testament writers believed the story of Noah and
the Flood?

If someone says that the story of Noah is just a myth, what
Bible people does he disagree with?

## Sumerian Noah

Archeologists have found stone tablets which contain a long and ancient
poem about Gilgamesh (GIL guh mesh). Gilgamesh was king of a city in
Sumer, the first empire after the Flood. Sumer preceded Babylonia in the area
of the two rivers Tigris and Euphrates.

In the epic, Gilgamesh is a hero more than human; he becomes godlike,
as often happens in ancient stories. He traveled through many dangers and
battles to find his ancestor Utnapishtim who had reached immortality. Once
Gilgamesh arrived, Utnapishtim told him of the time
when the gods declared they would destroy men by
drowning them all. But one god warned Utnapishtim
to build a boat. He did, and this portion of the epic
tells what happened next.

> Epic: Long poem,
> usually centered upon
> the achievements of a
> great hero.

### Gilgamesh Epic

*What I had, I loaded thereon,*
*The whole harvest of life*
*I caused to embark within the vessel;*
*All my family and relations,*
*The beasts of the field,*
*The cattle of the field,*
*The craftsmen,*
*I made them all embark.*
*I entered the vessel*
*And closed the door . . .*
*From the foundations of heaven*
*A black cloud arose . . .*
*All that is bright*
*Is turned into darkness,*
*The brother seeth the brother no more*
*For six days and nights*
*Winds and flood marched on,*
*The hurricane subdued the land.*
*When the seventh day dawned*
*The hurricane was abated—the flood*
*Which had waged war like an army;*
*The sea was stilled,*
*The ill wind was calmed,*
*The flood ceased.*
*I beheld the sea, its voice was silent*
*And all mankind was turned into mud!*
*As high as the roofs reached the swamp! . . .*
*Twelve measures away an island emerged;*
*Unto mount Nitsir came the vessel,*
*Mount Nitsir held the vessel*
*And let it not budge . . .*
*When the seventh day came*
*I sent forth a dove, I released it;*
*It went, the dove, it came back,*
*As there was no place, it came back.*
*I sent forth a swallow, I released it;*
*It went, the swallow, it came back.*
*I sent forth a crow, I released it;*
*It went, the crow,*
*And beheld the subsiding of the waters;*
*It eats, it splashes about, it caws,*
*It comes not back.*

A fragment of the Gilgamesh epic written in cuneiform.

Translated by Delaporte, quoted in *The Sumerians* by C. Leonard Woolley, pp. 123, 124.

Many history books say that since the Gilgamesh epic predated Moses by hundreds of years, Moses must have copied from it when he wrote Genesis. Can you give a better explanation for the Flood story in Genesis?

Almost all peoples of the world have an old story of a Flood that destroyed all mankind. Why do you think this is so?

## Chinese Noah

The ancient Chinese people arrived in their land not long after everybody scattered from Babel. At that time they still remembered the true history of creation, the garden of Eden, the Flood, and the tower of Babel. And for nearly 2000 years they worshiped one God, Shangti, who created everything.

In those early days somebody had to make a new writing system to go with the new language they had after Babel. Now, what would you do if that were your job? You have no letters yet, and no history of writing by sounds. All you know is something about writing by pictures. And today you must decide how the school children will learn to write boat. A big boat.

Here's what an ancient Chinese did. He started with the symbol for vessel, or container. That is shown on the left below. Next, the symbol for eight. And next, a mouth. A mouth stands for a person even in our language, as when we say a family has eight mouths to feed.

vessel            eight            mouth

The inventor was obviously thinking of the most famous big boat he knew, which was Noah's with eight people on it. He put together vessel, eight and people as shown below. And that meant boat.

boat

Information from *The Discovery of Genesis* by C.H. Kang and Ethel R. Nelson, p.95.

Why do you suppose that peoples, like the Chinese, lose their memory of God and true history after many generations?

Who are some individuals who helped pass the knowledge

of God along to you? Think of the generation just before you and of generations long ago.

What might happen to our society if we lose our memory of the God who created and who judged the world with a Flood?

What can you do to help the next generation?

# *Further Study*

**1. Correlated Readings.** Below are two suggested readings which correlate with Noah's book. The first is easier, narrative reading, and the second is advanced verse-by-verse study.

*a)* Adam and His Kin by Ruth Beechick, chapters 7 and 8.

*b)* The Genesis Record by Henry Morris, pages 151 to 178.

**2. Arithmetic Problems.** You can do some arithmetic to show when certain Flood time events happened. (One route to obtaining each answer is given at the bottom of this page, but other routes are possible.)

*a)* Did the Flood come in the year that Methuselah died? Use the numbers in 5:25-29 and 7:6 to check this out.

*b)* Lamech was Noah's father. Did he perish in the Flood or did he die before it came? Use the numbers in 5:28-31 and 7:6 to figure out.

*c)* In what year of Noah's life was Shem born? Use 7:6 and 11:10 to figure out. (Add this information to your genealogy list, which you will need for a project in the unit on Terah's book.)

*d)* In Hebrew writing, the letters were used for numerals as well as for words, something like Roman numerals. To learn how that works, you can try this activity with the English alphabet.

First, write the alphabet in columns. Then after the letters a to i write the numeric values 1 to 9. After the letters j to r, write the numeric values 10 to 90. After the rest of the letters, write 100, 200 and so forth. Now you can calculate the total value of the letters in your name and in other people's names.

**3. Writing.** Think of what you know about the world before the Flood and talk with someone about it. Then write one to three paragraphs explaining what life might have been like in those times. Or if you prefer, write a fictional story of someone who lived in those times.

Answer 1: 187 years to Lamech's birth plus 182 years to Noah's birth plus 600 years to the Flood equals 969, Methuselah's age at death.

Answer 2: 182 years to Noah's birth plus 600 years to the Flood equals 782 years. But Lamech lived only 777 years.

Answer 3: Noah was 600 years old at the Flood, thus 602 years old when Shem was 100. Subtract and find that Noah was 502 years old at Shem's birth.

# Unit IV

## Book of the Sons of Noah

"And Noah builded an altar unto the LORD . . . and offered burnt offerings on the altar" (Genesis 8:20). From a printed book, 1675, by Athanasius Kircher.

# *Scripture Text*

## Book of the Sons of Noah

**Genesis 6:9b** Noah was a just man *and* perfect in his generations, *and* Noah walked with God. **10** And Noah begat three sons, Shem, Ham, and Japheth. **11** The earth also was corrupt before God, and the earth was filled with violence. **12** And God looked upon the earth, and, behold, it was corrupt; for all flesh had corrupted his way upon the earth. **13** And God said unto Noah, The end of all flesh is come before me; for the earth is filled with violence through them; and, behold, I will destroy them with the earth. **14** Make thee an ark of gopher wood; rooms shalt thou make in the ark, and shalt pitch it within and without with pitch. **15** And this *is the fashion* which thou shalt make it *of*: The length of the ark *shall be* three hundred cubits, the breadth of it fifty cubits, and the height of it thirty cubits. **16** A window shalt thou make to the ark, and in a cubit shalt thou finish it above; and the door of the ark shalt thou set in the side thereof; *with* lower, second, and third *stories* shalt thou make it. **17** And, behold, I, even I, do bring a flood of waters upon the earth, to destroy all flesh, wherein is the breath of life, from under heaven; *and* every thing that *is* in the earth shall die. **18** But with thee will I establish my covenant; and thou shalt come into the ark, thou, and thy sons, and thy wife, and thy sons' wives with thee. **19** And of every living thing of all flesh, two of every *sort* shalt thou bring into the ark, to keep *them* alive with thee; they shall be male and female. **20** Of fowls after their kind, and of cattle after their kind, of every creeping thing of the earth after his kind, two of every *sort* shall come unto thee, to keep *them* alive. **21** And take thou unto thee of all food that is eaten, and thou shalt gather *it* to thee; and it shall be for food for thee, and for them. **22** Thus did Noah; according to all that God commanded him, so did he.

**7:1** And the Lord said unto Noah, Come thou and all thy house into the ark; for thee have I seen righteous before me in this generation. **2** Of every clean beast thou shalt take to thee by sevens, the male and his female: and of beasts that *are* not clean by two, the male and his female. **3** Of fowls also of the air by sevens, the male and the female; to keep seed alive upon the face of all the earth. **4** For yet seven days, and I will cause it to rain upon the earth forty days and forty nights; and every living substance that I have made will I destroy from off the face of the earth. **5** And Noah did according unto all that the Lord commanded him. **6** And Noah *was* six hundred years old when the flood of waters was upon the earth. **7** And Noah went in, and his sons, and his wife, and his sons' wives with him, into the ark, because of the waters of the flood. **8** Of clean beasts, and of beasts that *are* not clean, and of fowls, and of every thing that creepeth upon the earth, **9** There went in two and two unto Noah into the ark, the male and the female, as God had commanded Noah. **10** And it came to pass after seven days, that the waters of the flood were upon the earth. **11** In the six hundredth year of Noah's life, in the second month, the seventeenth day of the month, the same day were all the fountains of the great deep broken up, and the windows of heaven were opened. **12** And the rain was upon the earth forty days and forty nights. **13** In the selfsame day entered Noah, and Shem, and Ham, and Japheth, the sons of Noah, and Noah's wife, and the three wives of his sons with them, into the ark; **14** They, and every beast after his kind, and all the cattle after their kind, and every creeping thing that creepeth upon the earth after his kind, and every fowl after his kind, every bird of every sort. **15** And they went in unto Noah into the ark, two and two of all flesh, wherein *is* the breath of life. **16** And they that went in, went in male and female of all flesh, as God had commanded him: and the Lord shut him in. **17** And the flood was forty days upon the earth; and the waters increased, and bare up the ark, and it was lift up above the earth. **18** And the waters prevailed, and were increased greatly upon the earth; and the ark went upon the face of the waters. **19** And the waters prevailed exceedingly upon the earth; and all the high hills, that *were* under the whole heaven, were covered. **20** Fifteen cubits upward did the waters prevail; and the mountains were covered. **21** And all flesh died that moved upon the earth, both of fowl, and of cattle, and of beast, and of every creeping thing that creepeth upon the earth, and every man: **22** All in whose nostrils *was* the breath of life, of all that *was* in the dry *land*, died. **23** And every living substance was destroyed which was upon the face of the ground, both man, and cattle, and the creeping things, and the fowl of the heaven; and they were destroyed from the earth: and Noah only remained *alive*, and they that *were* with him in the ark. **24** And the waters prevailed upon the earth an hundred and fifty days.

**8:1** And God remembered Noah, and every living thing, and all the cattle that *was* with him in the ark: and God made a wind to pass over the earth, and the waters assuaged; **2** The fountains also of the deep and the windows of heaven were stopped, and the rain from heaven was restrained; **3** And the waters returned from off the earth continually: and after the end of the hundred and fifty days the waters were abated. **4** And the ark rested in the seventh month, on the seventeenth day of the month, upon the mountains of Ararat. **5** And the waters decreased continually until the tenth *month*: in the tenth month, on the first *day* of the month, were the tops of the mountains seen. **6** And it came to pass at the end of forty days, that Noah opened the window of the ark which he had made: **7** And he sent forth a raven, which went forth to and fro, until the waters were dried up from off the earth. **8** Also he sent forth a dove from him, to see if the waters were abated from off the face of the ground; **9** But the dove found no rest for the sole of her foot, and she returned unto him into the ark, for the waters *were* on the face of the whole earth: then he put forth his hand, and took her, and pulled her in unto him into the ark. **10** And he stayed yet other seven days; and again he sent forth the dove out of the ark; **11** And the dove came in to him in the evening; and, lo, in her mouth *was* an olive leaf pluckt off: so Noah knew that the waters were abated from off the earth. **12** And he stayed yet other seven days; and sent forth the dove; which returned not again unto him any more. **13** And it came to pass in the six hundredth and first year, in the first *month*, the first *day* of the month, the waters were dried up from off the earth: and Noah removed the covering of the ark, and looked, and, behold, the face of the ground was dry. **14** And in the second month, on the seven and twentieth day of the month, was the earth dried. **15** And God spake unto Noah, saying, **16** Go forth of the ark, thou, and thy wife, and thy sons, and thy sons' wives with thee. **17** Bring forth with thee every living thing that *is* with thee, of all flesh, *both* of fowl, and of cattle, and of every creeping thing that creepeth upon the earth; that they may breed abundantly in the earth, and be fruitful, and multiply upon the earth. **18** And Noah went forth, and his sons, and his wife, and his sons' wives with him: **19** Every beast, every creeping thing, and every fowl, *and* whatsoever creepeth upon the earth, after their kinds, went forth out of the ark. **20** And Noah builded an altar unto the Lord; and took of every clean beast, and of every clean fowl, and offered burnt offerings on the altar. **21** And the Lord smelled a sweet savour; and the Lord said in his heart, I will not again curse the ground any more for man's sake; for the imagination of man's heart *is* evil from his youth; neither will I again smite any more every thing living, as I have done. **22** While the earth remaineth, seedtime and harvest, and cold and heat, and summer and winter, and day and night shall not cease.

"I will not again curse the ground." On the contrary, God will restore the earth to its pre-Flood healthier condition. The great earthquakes, rainless years, and other upheavals described in Revelation will accomplish this. See *Creation and the Second Coming* by Henry Morris.

**9:1** And God blessed Noah and his sons, and said unto them, Be fruitful, and multiply, and replenish the earth. **2** And the fear of you and the dread of you shall be upon every beast of the earth, and upon every fowl of the air, upon all that moveth *upon* the earth, and upon all the fishes of the sea; into your hand are they delivered. **3** Every moving thing that liveth shall be meat for you; even as the green herb have I given you all things. **4** But flesh with the life thereof, *which* is the blood thereof, shall ye not eat. **5** And surely your blood of your lives will I require; at the hand of every beast will I require it, and at the hand of man; at the hand of every man's brother will I require the life of man. **6** Whoso sheddeth man's blood, by man shall his blood be shed: for in the image of God made he man. **7** And you, be ye fruitful, and multiply; bring forth abundantly in the earth, and multiply therein. **8** And God spake unto Noah, and to his sons with him, saying, **9** And I, behold, I establish my covenant with you, and with your seed after you; **10** And with every living creature that is with you, of the fowl, of the cattle, and of every beast of the earth with you; from all that go out of the ark, to every beast of the earth. **11** And I will establish my covenant with you, neither shall all flesh be cut off any more by the waters of a flood; neither shall there any more be a flood to destroy the earth. **12** And God said, This *is* the token of the covenant which I make between me and you and every living creature that is with you, for perpetual generations: **13** I do set my bow in the cloud, and it shall be for a token of a covenant between me and the earth. **14** And it shall come to pass, when I bring a cloud over the earth, that the bow shall be seen in the cloud: **15** And I will remember my covenant, which *is* between me and you and every living creature of all flesh; and the waters shall no more become a flood to destroy all flesh. **16** And the bow shall be in the cloud; and I will look upon it, that I may remember the everlasting covenant between God and every living

"And all flesh died that moved upon the earth" (Genesis 7:21).
Bible illustration by Gustave Doré, 1865.

creature of all flesh that is upon the earth. **17** And God said unto Noah, This *is* the token of the covenant, which I have established between me and all flesh that *is* upon the earth. **18** And the sons of Noah, that went forth of the ark, were Shem, and Ham, and Japheth: and Ham *is* the father of Canaan. **19** These *are* the three sons of Noah: and of them was the whole earth overspread. **20** And Noah began *to be* an husbandman, and he planted a vineyard: **21** And he drank of the wine, and was drunken; and he was uncovered within his tent. **22** And Ham, the father of Canaan, saw the nakedness of his father, and told his two brethren without. **23** And Shem and Japheth took a garment, and laid *it* upon both their shoulders, and went backward, and covered the nakedness of their father; and their faces *were* backward, and they saw not their father's nakedness. **24** And Noah awoke from his wine, and knew what his younger son had done unto him. **25** And he said, Cursed *be* Canaan; a servant of servants shall he be unto his brethren. **26** And he said, Blessed *be* the Lord God of Shem; and Canaan shall be his servant. **27** God shall enlarge Japheth, and he shall dwell in the tents of Shem; and Canaan shall be his servant. **28** And Noah lived after the flood three hundred and fifty years. **29** And all the days of Noah were nine hundred and fifty years: and he died.

**10:1** Now these *are* the generations of the sons of Noah, Shem, Ham, and Japheth . . .

ABOVE : The Great Architect of the Universe. This view of God was painted in a hand-illustrated Bible in France in the 1200s. The compass is large, like those in the Middle Ages. God traces out the limits of the universe. The earth is still without form, the firmament shows between the waters, and the heavenly lights can be seen.

DAY 1: God's arm stretched out over the watery globe. Angels watching.

DAY 2: God's hand in upper left. Outer water surrounds the earth.

DAY 3: God's hands again. The earth filled with colorful trees and plants.

DAY 4: Two great lights and the stars. Faces on sun and moon were added in the 1700s.

DAY 5: Fishes for the sea and birds for the sky, all under the hand of God.

DAY 6: Newly created man. Animals and plants shown, and an angel overhead.

DAY 7: God seated in majesty, resting, surrounded by angels and earth's creatures.

Gate of a Maori village today. These people have an oral tradition that the Supreme God has no beginning, is everlasting, is over all things, and is the source of all knowledge and thought.

ABOVE: From a hand copied Hebrew Bible, Italy, 1448. This is from the first page of Genesis, showing the first word, beginning. The Hebrews did not have capitals, so instead of elaborately decorating an initial letter as the Christians did, they embellished initial words.

ABOVE: ". . . a pure river of water of life, clear as crystal, proceeding out of the throne of God and of the Lamb . . . and on either side of the river, was there the tree of life, which bare twelve manner of fruits, and yielded her fruit every month: and the leaves of the tree were for the healing of the nations" (Revelation 22:1-2).

"And the Lord God planted a garden eastward in Eden; and there he put the man whom he had formed" (Genesis 2:8).

The Garden of Eden as painted in the 1600s by Jan van Kessel of Flanders, a country that encompassed what is now western Belgium and a bit of northern France. Van Kessel is known for miniature still-life paintings with exquisite detail, which can be seen here in the fruit, flowers and the living creatures. Adam and Eve are in miniature in the middle distance. Calm blues and greens lend a feeling of peace to the picture.

Shows the splendid design and layout of the great east window of York Minster in York, England. One of the finest stained-glass treasures anywhere, from the Middle Ages. The top row shows scenes from the creation of the world and the fall of man into sin. See pages 66 and 67 for details of the creation panels.

Brachiosaurus (bra ke o SAW rus)

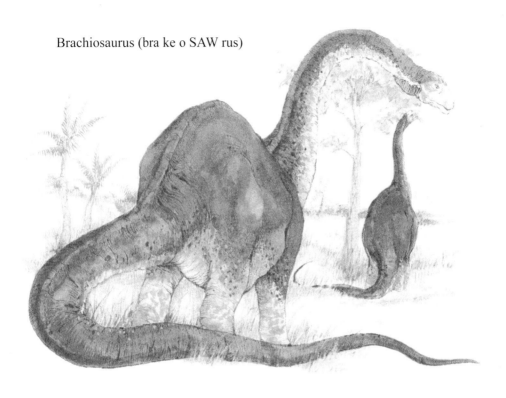

Paleoscincus (pay le o SKING kus)

LEFT: Building the Tower of Babel, by an unknown artist about A. D. 1000. Do we see some humor in this, as though the workmen cannot communicate about their differing styles of building?

Excavating Ur, the home of Terah. Terah's son Abram grew up in this city and lived there until God called him to a new land. In those days the Euphrates River ran by the city and it was not desert, but one of the richest and most beautiful cities in Sumer. It was discovered by Sir Henry Rawlinson in 1854 and excavated by Leonard Woolley in 1922-34.

CASPIAN SEA

- 40°

- 35°

- 30°

UR

PERSIAN
GULF

## Map Activities

1. Find Mount Ararat, where the ark landed.

2. Find Babylon (originally Babel), where the people rebelled against God.

3. Which of the two landmarks above is closest to the 40th parallel? (You will read about this 40th parallel in the topic "History in the Stars.")

4. Trace a route that settlers may have taken to gradually move from Mount Ararat to Shinar (Babylonia). Notice that verse 11:2 says they came "from the east."

5. Archeologists have found reference to a town named Aratta, but they have not discovered the town. Do you have a guess where it might be?

6. Find the Nile River and Egypt. Which branch of Noah's family settled there and in other parts of Africa?

7. Find the large Arabian peninsula east of Egypt. The Arabians there are mostly descended from which son of Noah?

8. Find the Caucasus Mountains. Does this give you a hint as to why some people are called Caucasian? Are you a Caucasian?

9. People who went north of the Caucasus Mountains or who moved westward became various peoples of Europe. These are the descendants of which son of Noah?

10. Find Ur, the town where archeologists think Abram grew up.

11. Find Canaan, the land God promised to Abram and his descendants.

12. Make some copies of the blank map in the appendix (p. 124) and practice writing from memory all the cities and geographical features you would like to remember.

*"And God made . . . the stars also" (from Genesis 1:16).*

This sky map of the northern hemisphere is from an atlas produced by the Otten family in Amsterdam in 1745. It includes many constellations from the most ancient times, as well as a few newer ones. The ancient sky pictures and their stories were similar the world over, which indicates that they had one point of origin. It is possible that the star stories just after the Flood were true stories of the seed of the woman crushing the serpent, and others, but they were corrupted into pagan versions, institutionalized at Babel, and then spread from there. This would have begun during the generations listed in Terah's genealogy.

"And God created great dinosaurs . . . which the waters brought forth abundantly" (Genesis 1:21a).

The Vikings built dragon-ships, possibly to scare off the great sea dragons which still roamed the northern seas in their days.

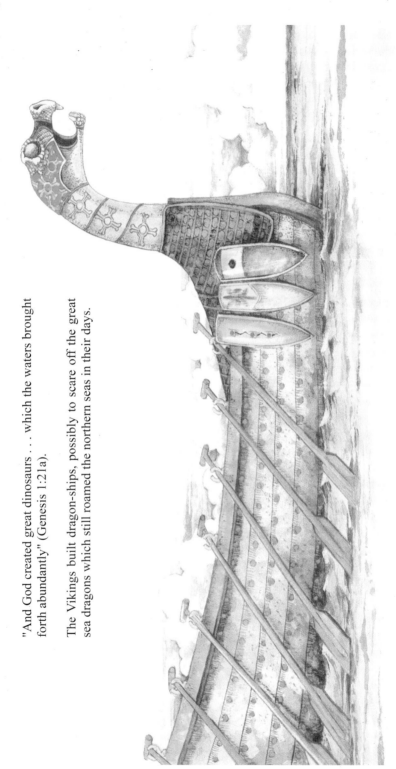

### Giants and Dragons

"There were giants in the earth in those days; and also after that" (Genesis 6:4a).

This is an ancient picture of King Arthur meeting a giant who is roasting meat. Though some legends are told about King Arthur, he was a real king, and his king line is traced back through Javan and Japheth to Noah. The giants were said to have come to England about 2000 years before Christ. They came from Africa and were descendants of Ham. By King Arthur's time only a few giants remained.

Why is King Arthur often treated by historians as a legend instead of history? For the same reason they treat Noah as legend. For proofs of the historicity of Arthur and others, see *After the Flood* by Bill Cooper.

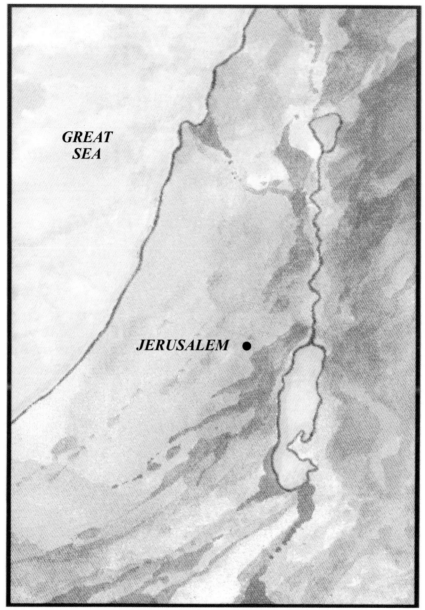

*GREAT SEA*

*JERUSALEM* ●

Canaan, which became Israel, was at the east end of the Mediterranean Sea (the Great Sea). The geography is divided into three parallel strips running north to south: the coastal plain to the west, the mountain ranges (including the Hills of Galilee), and the valley on the eastern border. The small lake to the north is the Sea of Galilee (which in earlier times was known as Chinnereth). The Jordan River runs south to the Dead Sea, the lowest body of water on earth.

# *Scripture Study*

**Read** this book of the sons of Noah. Some of this is from the very ancient log, or diary, which Noah's family kept aboard ship. Notice its numerous details which they must have written during their year-long voyage. The latter part of this book tells of Noah becoming drunk and of him pronouncing blessings and a curse upon his descendants.

**Compare** 9:3 with 1:29. What different diet instructions did God give before the Flood and after the Flood?

**Find** a part that answers each of the following questions. Your family or group can do this together, with each finder reading the part aloud. Since the Noah's ark story is retold in many books, we sometimes hear incorrect ideas about it, so it is worthwhile to look closely at the eyewitness account.

Who made the plan for the ark?
What did God say would die in the Flood?
What did die in the Flood?
How old was Noah when he entered the ark?
How old was Noah when he exited the ark?
What part shows that God brought the animals?
Where did the Flood waters come from?
What date is given for the family's entrance into the ark?
What date is given for leaving the ark? (Mark these dates
    for later use.)

<blockquote>
Several dates are in the story, so check the context
carefully to get the right dates.
</blockquote>

What is an example of information that sounds like it came
    from records kept aboard ship?
What did God say about relations between people and
    animals after the Flood?
What are God's instructions about capital punishment?
In Noah's prophecies whom did he curse?
In Noah's prophecies whom did he bless?

**Make up** more questions to ask each other.

**Circle** the word *seven* several places in the story. (You can use these for one of the topic studies later.)

**Tell** the story of the Flood as accurately as you can. There probably are too many details to include all, but you could prepare a list of important ideas, such as why the Flood came, where so much water came from, about how long the Flood lasted, how Noah knew when to disembark, his sacrifice, and God's promise. Then use the list, if you wish, to keep your story in order.

**Memorize** either 8:22 or 9:13. These are two promises that God made to mankind immediately after the Flood. (If you memorize 9:13, be sure you know what the covenant is—a promise that God will never again destroy the earth with a Flood.)

# *Topic Study*

## What Is a Mabbul?

*Mabbul* (mah BOOL) is the Hebrew word in 6:17 where God says He will bring a "flood of waters" upon the earth. The King James translators knew this word meant something more than an ordinary local flood, so they called it a *flood of waters*. *Mabbul* includes the idea of destruction, and it could be translated "water cataclysm."

The New Testament uses the Greek word *kataklusmos* (kat a klooz MOSE) for Noah's Flood. Both *mabbul* and *kataklusmos* speak only of Noah's Flood. A different word is used for the flood that beat the house upon the rock and for other floods in the Bible. (In this book we capitalize *Flood* when it means *mabbul*.)

The *mabbul* happened only once in history, and God promised it would never happen again. That worldwide cataclysm caused great upheaval of the earth's crust; it laid down many layers of sediment; it formed millions of fossils; it thrust up mountains. The earth's geography was drastically changed in Noah's 600th year.

Strangely, some people, even Bible believers, think that Noah's Flood was not worldwide, but was only local in the Middle East. If they would stop to think, they'd see that that means God broke His promise, because God promised He would not bring a Flood like Noah's again. They should know, then, that Noah's Flood was not like floods that continue to occur in history.

Does God break promises?

Did God promise never again to bring a Flood to destroy the earth?

How does God's promise help you to know whether Noah's Flood was local or worldwide?

A feature called the Mid-Oceanic Ridge runs through the Atlantic and around the earth—an evidence of major upheaval in earth's history. See *In the Beginning* by Walt Brown for more information on this.

If a Bible believer tells you he thinks Noah's Flood was not worldwide, how could you use God's promise to respond to him?

## Ignorant Scoffers

The apostle Peter said that in the last days people will scoff at Noah's Flood. We must be living in the last days, because people all around us deny that the Flood ever happened.

Evidence of the Flood is everywhere, so why do people deny it? Because they choose to be ignorant. They are willingly ignorant, Peter said.

Why are they willingly ignorant? Well, if they admit that God judged the world once, then they have to admit that He can judge it again. They'd rather not think about judgment to come and they'd rather not get right with God. So they choose to believe that the world has always continued as it is, without the Flood in its history.

Peter wrote about this in II Peter 3:3-7.

Does your family know anybody who scoffs at Noah's Flood?

What New Testament writer does a scoffer disagree with?

If you were talking with a scoffer, could you explain one or more evidences of the Flood which we can still see today? Or do you have a book or article to offer the person?

## What Does Seven Mean?

Bible scholars say that the Hebrew word seven is from a root which means *full*, *satisfied*, or *have enough of*. An example of this meaning in Scripture is that God rested on the seventh day from the full and complete creation.

In the Flood account, Noah's sons wrote that God told Noah to board the animals and enter the ark, because the rain would begin in seven days. And the Flood began exactly seven days after that warning. This may indicate that the sin of the world had reached its fullness and God's judgment had to fall.

Also, God told Noah to take seven pairs of each clean beast. This is the full amount that were saved on the ark. This number seven and other numbers, too, often have significant meanings in Scripture.

Can you name two sevens in the Flood story and their possible meanings?

Can you name a seven in the creation story and its meaning?

Can you think of any other sevens in the Bible and their possible meanings?

# What Happened to the Dinosaurs?

Everybody wants to know the answer to the dinosaur question. Scientists have lots of guesses, like disease, cosmic rays from a supernova, and changes in the magnetic field of earth. The guess that seems most reasonable is that climate changed drastically so there was not enough vegetation to support these large creatures.

That leads to the next question, which is: Why did the climate change? Scientists who put Noah's Flood into the history of the earth have a good explanation for that. Because the protective canopy of water fell to earth, and polar ice caps formed and the ice age came, the dinosaurs lost their lush habitat with plenty of food and warmth.

Some dinosaurs would have survived the Flood, because God brought every kind of animal to Noah. Small, young land dinosaurs probably came to the ark, and some sea dinosaurs could survive in the water. So while many dinosaurs became fossils during the Flood and the upheavals which followed, some lived in the new climate for a time. But most of these died out because the new earth was not at all like the old earth where dinosaurs thrived.

> **Dino-** from Greek, meaning terrifying or frightful.
> **-saur** used in the names of extinct reptiles. Greek: lizards.

Job lived in a time not long after the Flood, maybe about 300 years after, and he saw dinosaurs. Here is his description of a monster with a tail like no animal we see today; it was as thick as a cedar tree. It sounds much like a land dinosaur, perhaps a Brachiosaurus (bray ke o SAW rus).

> *"He moveth his tail like a cedar ... his bones are like bars of iron. . . . he drinketh up a river . . . his nose pierceth through snares"* (from Job 40:15-24). [see page 71 bottom]

Job described another dinosaur which probably lived in or near water, and which had an impenatrable armor of scales. It's hard to make a good guess about this dinosaur, because we don't usually find fossils of skin and scales, but only bones. Shown here is a modern drawing of a Paleoscincus (pay le o SKING kus), which does have scales, and spikes too. [see page 71 bottom]

> *"Canst thou draw out the leviathan with an hook? . . . His scales are his pride. . . . one is so near to another, that no air can come between them. . . . The arrow cannot make him flee: slingstones are turned with him into stubble"* (from Job 41).

The literature and drawings from many countries indicate that a few dinosaurs survived much later than Job's time—into the Middle Ages. These stories are different from the mythological serpent stories involving gods and cosmic battles, which are a dim memory of the serpent of Eden. These stories seem to feature real human heroes who have become legendary. Here is one such story from England.

## Sir George and the Dragon

Once in a country town a dreadful dragon so terrorized the people that many ran away from their homes. Others fled to the king's castle for safety within its walls. Brave princess Una rode off to fetch a young knight named Sir George.

As the two neared the castle all the people cheered and clapped for the champion who would fight the dragon. The dragon, too, saw the shining armor and filled the air with hideous roaring. Then it came down a hillside to meet the knight. After a fearsome battle that lasted about three days, Sir George succeeded in killing the dragon.

Then Sir George married the beautiful princess and everybody lived happily.

Sir George was later called Saint George because of his deeds.

Another dragon-fighting hero was Beowulf. His name means *bear*, which was *beewolf* in his Anglo-Saxon language. Bears got that name by raiding beehives. In literature books Beowulf is always called fiction, but characters in the story are actual historical figures, and Beowulf himself was a king in Denmark from A.D. 533 to A.D. 583. He killed the monster Grendel as a young man in A.D. 515. (See *After the Flood* by Bill Cooper for more historical information about Beowulf.)

Not only are the people and practically all historical details real and verifiable, so also are the scary creatures. Grendel himself was described in the original language as greedy, ravenous, the walker in darkness, the terrifying ugly one, and other terms that seem to describe a real rather than a fantastic creature. Beowulf conquered him by getting too close for the long jaws to grab him, and with the great strength he was known for, tearing off Grendel's small forearm, his weakest feature, so that the monster bled to death. This excerpt from the epic poem tells of the killing.

## Beowulf

Over the misty moor
From the dark and dripping caves of his grim lair,
Grendel with fierce ravenous stride came stepping.
A shadow under the pale moon he moved,
That fiend from hell, foul enemy of God,
Toward Heorot. He beheld it from afar, the gleaming roof
Towering high to heaven. His tremendous hands
Struck the studded door, wrenched it from the hinges
Till the wood splintered and the bolts burst apart.
Angrily he prowled over the polished floor,

A terrible light in his eyes—a torch flaming!
As he scanned the warriors, deep-drugged in sleep,
Loud loud he laughed, and pouncing on the nearest
Tore him limb from limb and swallowed him whole,
Sucking the blood in streams, crunching the bones,
Half-gorged, his gross appetite still unslaked,
Greedily he reached his hand for the next—little reckoning
For Beowulf. The youth clutched it and firmly grappled.
Such torture as this the fiend had never known.
In mortal fear, he was minded to flee to his lair,
But Beowulf prisoned him fast. . . .
No manmade weapon might avail. Alone, Beowulf
Tore Grendel's arm from his shoulder asunder,
Wrenched it from the root while the tough sinews cracked.
And the monster roared in anguish, well knowing
That deadly was the wound and his mortal days ended.
Wildly lamenting, away into the darkness he limped,
Over the misty moor to his gloomy home.
But the hero rejoiced in his triumph and wildly waved
In the air his blood-soaked trophy.

Did Grendel look something like this modern drawing of a Tyrannosaurus  (ty RAN o SAW rus)? This creature is said to be a meat eater with large jaws and teeth, who walked on strong back legs and had small, weak forearms.

From ancient Babylon several drawings have been found similar to that reproduced here. The creature has small forearms and, though the drawing is stylized, it may be showing the man conquering in the same way that

Beowulf conquered his dragon, by twisting off the forearm. The man's bulging muscles show that he is a hero known for strength.

Today there still may be a few remnants of dinosaurs. We hear occasional reports of sightings. Could the Loch Ness monster have been a landlocked sea dinosaur? From a fuzzy underwater photo, some have identified it as Elasmosaurus (ee LASS mo SAW rus).

In 1977 a Japanese fishing vessel caught a smelly monster which had been dead for about a month. They photographed it, took samples, and then dropped it into the sea again so they could fill their vessel with fish. After much study, a number of scientists concluded that it was a plesiosaur (PLE ze uh SAWR). Japanese newspapers gave wide publicity to this remarkable discovery and the government commemorated it with a postage stamp. But in America the media largely ignored it. This is what they usually do with a discovery that upsets the theory of evolution.

Explain what could have happened to dinosaurs during and after the Flood.

Evolutionists believe that dinosaurs died out long before man appeared. Explain how this gives them a big problem with a discovery like the Japanese fishermen made.

## Where Is the Ark?

Until modern times, people always seemed to know that the ark was on top of Mount Ararat. A famous explorer, Marco Polo, traveled from Italy to China in A.D. 1275. In his report of the trip, he wrote the following.

It must be known, then, that from the creation of Adam to the present day, no man . . . ever saw or inquired into so many and such great things as Marco Polo . . .

In the central part of Armenia stands an exceedingly large and high mountain, upon which, it is said, the Ark of Noah rested, and for this reason it is termed the Mountain of the Ark. The circuit of its base cannot be compassed in less than two days. The ascent is impracticable on account of the snow towards the summit, which never melts, but goes on increasing by each successive fall.

(*The Travels of Marco Polo*, Random House, 1953, p. 25.)

Today the mountain lies within the borders of Turkey, which is just south of Armenia. Both before and after Marco Polo there were many reports of the ark.

View from Ahora Gorge near the top of rugged Mount Ararat.
Photo by Dr. John Morris.

In the 1700s, a dictionary of Bible history contained a map of the Middle East with a drawing of the mountain and the ark upon it. In the first century after Christ, lived the historian Josephus, who wrote this account.

Then the ark settled on a mountain-top in Armenia . . . The Armenians call that spot the Landing-place, for it was there that the ark came safe to land, and they show the relics of it to this day.

A historian from ancient Babylonia wrote that the ship grounded in Armenia and that part of it remained in the mountains there in his day, and people scraped pitch from it to use for magic amulets that heal. His history adds that after the Flood people traveled from the mountain to Babylon (formerly Sumer) and built cities and temples there. The Bible says exactly the same thing; it calls the land of settlement Shinar.

During the 1800s and into the 1900s we have numerous reports of people sighting the ark from a plane or helicopter, or even climbing up to and into the ark. At the time of this writing, the ark, or what remains of it, seems to be under snow and ice year round, so it has not been visible in recent years. We have lost track of its exact location on the rugged and dangerous mountain, so people now refer to it as "lost." Many people who don't believe the Bible also don't believe any of the other reports about the ark.

What did the Armenians tell Marco Polo?

What did Josephus say that people did with the ark?

What did the Babylonian historian say that people did with
the ark?

Would you like to read about expeditions to Mount Ararat?
Or go on an expedition?

## What Became Of Noah's Curse?

GREAT
SEA

JERUSALEM

Noah's prophetic curse on Canaan, the son of Ham, is found in 9:25-27. Noah said that Canaan will be a servant to Shem.

Did this come true? Yes. Centuries later, Shem's descendants (Israelites) entered the promised land with General Joshua, and they had to conquer and destroy the Canaanites. One group of Canaanites tricked the Israelites into promising not to kill them. So the Israelites said they could be slaves, instead. That whole story is told in Joshua 9. Here's part of it.

Canann, which became Israel, was at the east end of the Mediterranean Sea (Great Sea).

Let them live; but let them be hewers of wood and drawers of water unto all the congregation; as the princes had promised them. And Joshua called for them, and he spake unto them, saying . . . Now therefore ye are cursed, and there shall none of you be freed from being bondmen, and hewers of wood and drawers of water for the house of my God (from Joshua 9:21-23).

The other side of Noah's curse is that Shem's family was blessed, and Japheth's family would get into the tent and share the blessing. That is a simple picture of the history of Noah's sons, down to our time and even into the future.

From Shem's family came the Israelites. They were blessed with the promised land in Old Testament times, and they will be blessed to dwell in the land forever, and God will be their God (Ezekiel 37:21-28 and other prophets). Through Shem's family came the greatest blessing of all time—Jesus. After Jesus, Christianity spread mostly westward from Israel and became strong in the western nations, Japheth's descendants. That was Japheth coming into the tent with Shem and sharing his blessings.

What was the prophetic curse on Canaan?

How did the prophecy come true?

Has Shem been blessed in history? Will he be blessed in the future? How?

How does Japheth share Shem's blessing in history?

# *Further Study*

**1. Correlated Readings.** Below are two suggested readings which correlate with the book of the sons of Noah. The first is easier, narrative reading, and the second is advanced verse-by-verse study.

*a) Adam and His Kin* by Ruth Beechick, chapters 9 to 13.

*b) The Genesis Record* by Henry Morris, pages 178 to 246.

**2. Other Readings.** Excellent books are available on the two topics mentioned below.

*a) Flood Science.* Scientists who hold the creation view of origins, also factor a worldwide Flood into the history of the earth. The research and writing of these people is a wonderful blessing for us all. Some topics to read about are: how the Flood accounts for earth's geologic formations, how it accounts for fossils, how and when the ice age appeared, changes in the water cycle at the time of the Flood, and possible reasons for the longevity of human life in earth's early years. New publications are appearing all the time, so it is easy to keep up with developments in this field.

If you have not read any recent creationist books, you have a treat in store for you, especially if you've seen only our society's evolutionary textbooks, TV shows, and other media. You'll have your mind stimulated as seldom happens in these days of media saturation. Some of these science books are listed in the bibliography.

*b) Search for Noah's Ark.* A few good books have been written also on this topic, as well as some undependable, sensational ones. Some are listed in the bibliography, but watch for any new, breaking news on this search.

**3. Writing.** Here are several ideas for writing projects.

*a)* Write a report on your choice of topic from the readings suggested above.

*b)* If you read about a new sighting of Noah's ark, write an article or letter to the editor in order to get the information into your local paper. Spread the word, also, if there's a sighting of a dinosaur or any breaking scientific news that supports the biblical view of world history.

*c)* Write an essay explaining why you believe in a worldwide Flood in Noah's time. Or why you don't, if that's your view.

*d)* If you want to study details of the Flood year, you could write a log or diary in which you tell the most interesting happenings.

**4. Arithmetic**. How long were Noah and his family on the ark? First you need to find the Scripture portions which tell the dates that Noah's family entered and left the ark. You may have marked these earlier during study of the Scripture text. Then subtract to find the total time.

To subtract dates, start with three columns for the date of leaving, which is the latest of the two dates:

year 601      month 2      day 27

Beneath those numbers write the date they entered the ark. Then subtract. It's an easy problem; no borrowing. The true answer may be slightly different from this, because the year in the pre-Flood world may have been exactly 12 months of 30 days each, and the catastrophe may have changed that slightly. (See chapter 11 of *Adam and His Kin* for thoughts on this calendar problem.)

From a hand painted manuscript,
France, about 1280.

# Unit V

## *Book of Shem*

(See Building the Tower of Babel painting on page 72)

# *Scripture Text*

## Book of Shem

**Genesis 10:1b** . . . and unto them were sons born after the flood. **2** The sons of Japheth; Gomer, and Magog, and Madai, and Javan, and Tubal, and Meshech, and Tiras. **3** And the sons of Gomer; Ashkenaz, and Riphath, and Togarmah. **4** And the sons of Javan; Elishah, and Tarshish, Kittim, and Dodanim. **5** By these were the isles of the Gentiles divided in their lands; every one after his tongue, after their families, in their nations. **6** And the sons of Ham; Cush, and Mizraim, and Phut, and Canaan. **7** And the sons of Cush; Seba, and Havilah, and Sabtah, and Raamah, and Sabtechah: and the sons of Raamah; Sheba, and Dedan. **8** And Cush begat Nimrod: he began to be a mighty one in the earth. **9** He was a mighty hunter before the Lord: wherefore it is said, Even as Nimrod the mighty hunter before the Lord. **10** And the beginning of his kingdom was Babel, and Erech, and Accad, and Calneh, in the land of Shinar. **11** Out of that land went forth Asshur [or: he went forth to Asshur.], and builded Nineveh, and the city Rehoboth, and Calah, **12** And Resen between Nineveh and Calah: the same *is* a great city. **13** And Mizraim begat Ludim, and Anamim, and Lehabim, and Naphtuhim, **14** And Pathrusim, and Casluhim, (out of whom came Philistim,) and Caphtorim. **15** And Canaan begat Sidon his first born, and Heth, **16** And the Jebusite, and the Amorite, and the Girgasite, **17** And the Hivite, and the Arkite, and the Sinite, **18** And the Arvadite, and the Zemarite, and the Hamathite: and afterward were the families of the Canaanites spread abroad. **19** And the border of the Canaanites was from Sidon, as thou comest to Gerar, unto Gaza; as thou goest, unto Sodom, and Gomorrah, and Admah, and Zeboim, even unto Lasha. **20** These *are* the sons of Ham, after their families, after their tongues, in their countries, *and* in their nations. **21** Unto Shem also, the father of all the children of Eber, the brother of Japheth the elder, even to him were *children* born. **22** The children of Shem; Elam, and Asshur, and Arphaxad, and Lud, and Aram. **23** And the children of Aram; Uz, and Hul, and Gether, and Mash. **24** And Arphaxad begat Salah; and Salah begat Eber. **25** And unto Eber were born two sons: the name of one *was* Peleg; for in his days was the earth divided; and his brother's name was Joktan. **26** And Joktan begat Almodad, and Sheleph, and Hazarmaveth, and Jerah, **27** And Hadoram, and Uzal, and Diklah, **28** And Obal, and Abimael, and Sheba, **29** And Ophir, and Havilah, and Jobab: all these *were* the sons of Joktan. **30** And their dwelling was from Mesha, as thou goest unto Sephar a mount of the east. **31** These *are* the sons of Shem, after their families, after their tongues, in their lands, after their nations. **32** These *are* the families of the sons of Noah, after their generations, in their nations: and by these were the nations divided in the earth after the flood.

**11:1** And the whole earth was of one language, and of one speech. **2** And it came to pass, as they journeyed from the east, that they found a plain in the land of Shinar; and they dwelt there. **3** And they said one to another, Go to, let us make brick, and burn them thoroughly. And they had brick for stone, and slime had they for morter. **4** And they said, Go to, let us build us a city and a tower, whose top *may reach* unto heaven; and let us make us a name, lest we be scattered abroad upon the face of the whole earth. **5** And the Lord came down to see the city and the tower, which the children of men builded. **6** And the Lord said, Behold, the people is one, and they have all one language; and this they begin to do: and now nothing will be restrained from them, which they have imagined to do. **7** Go to, let us go down, and there confound their language, that they may not understand one another's speech. **8** So the Lord scattered them abroad from thence upon the face of all the earth: and they left off to build the city. **9** Therefore is the name of it called Babel; because the Lord did there confound the language of all the earth: and from thence did the Lord scatter them abroad upon the face of all the earth. **10** These *are* the generations of Shem . . .

Modern archeologists' idea of the tower of Babel. In Mesopotamia they find ruins of towers like this, called ziggurats.

# *Scripture Study*

**Read.** Shem's book is the best history we have from this period of time. Today's evolutionary historians make guesses about this time, that people lived in caves and gradually learned about fire and language and farming and metal. They think civilization began as primitive and slowly grew better.

But Shem's story is just the opposite. In his story, Noah and sons certainly knew how to build civilized towns as the population grew. But then came the Babel judgment and people scattered in small groups. Some of these groups probably lived in caves for a time then. The scattered people also had lost some of their language ability, and they couldn't write their new languages at first, so no one wrote much history for us. When they did start writing, they wrote the pagan, Satanic stories passed down by their ancestors from Babel. Only Shem's family kept alive God's side of the story.

Shem lived for 500 years after the Flood, so this is an eyewitness account of his own times. He wrote the best document there is about the origin of nations. And he wrote the important story of the tower of Babel. Moses put these writings into the book of Genesis and we can still read them today.

**Mark** an outline in the margin of your copy of Shem's book, using the guide below. Start by writing *Nations* at the beginning. Then you can write *Japheth*, *Ham* and *Shem* or their initials to label the sections for Noah's sons. Lastly you can label the story of Babel and its two parts.

> I. Table of Nations
>> A. Japheth's sons
>> B. Ham's sons
>> C. Shem's sons
> II. Tower of Babel
>> A. Sin
>> B. Judgment

List the descendants for one or more of Noah's sons, using names given in Shem's book. If you like, you can select the son you think you are descended from. Try to draw these in the form of a family tree, as shown in the sample below which shows one generation of Japheth's descendants.

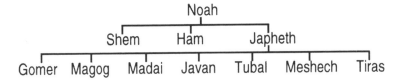

**Map Activities - See pages 74-75**

**Tell** the story of Babel to your father or to someone else who wants to listen. Prepare by reading Shem's story carefully. You might also practice and ask someone to help make sure you include everything and get the right order.

**Memorize** 10:32. This verse will help you remember the outline of Shem's book. The verse says that the families are listed by nations and that the nations were divided in the earth (because of Babel). Those are the two parts of Shem's book.

# *Topic Study*

## The Table of Nations

More and more historians are deciding that Genesis 10 is an important and useful ancient document. They call it the Table of Nations. The table has a section for each of the three sons of Noah. (See *After the Flood* by Bill Cooper.)

**Japheth** is the eldest (10:21), and we read about his families in verses 2-5. Seven sons of Japheth are listed, as well as some grandsons. These descendants spread mostly throughout Europe, and one branch in India. These Indian and European peoples and their languages are so similar that we refer to them as a group by the term Indo-European.

The Greeks claim Japheth as their forefather, through his son Javan. In fact, they worshipped Japheth as Iapetos, the son of heaven and earth. In Rome he was called Iupater, which in time became Jupiter.

Babel

Japheth's son Gomer dwelt in the northern lands (Ezekiel 38:6). Gomer's son Ashchenaz fathered the Germans, and the names Scandia and Saxony possibly also retain something of Ashchenaz in them. Gomer's son Riphath became the Paphlagonians who settled near the Black Sea, and may have given his name to Europe itself. Gomer's other son Togarmah became lost to history when the Assyrians conquered and dispersed them.

Japheth's sons spread mostly north and west.

A recent discovery has turned up some Gomerites in the Far East. They are the Miao mountain tribes of southwest China who claim to be descended from Japheth through Gomer. Here are some lines from their oral history which show these names.

The Patriarch Japhu
got the center of nations.
The son he begat
was the Patriarch Go-men.
(See Unit III for more of this Miao poem.)

Japheth's three sons, Magog, Meshech and Tubal are mentioned several times in the Old Testament, as well as the New. They founded Georgia and other northern countries, and gave their names to the Russian cities of Moscow and Tobolsk. Ezekiel prophecied against these and several other peoples and tells what they will do in the end times (Ezekiel 38-39). Some of these tribes moved west instead of north; the Irish Celts, for one group, traced their history back through Magog.

At least one son of Japheth did not travel far. He is Madai, who became the Medes that we read about in the Bible as part of the Medo-Persian kingdom.

Tiras's descendants were known in ancient times by several names, but always as invaders and pirates. Tiras was worshipped as Thor, the god of war. His name lives on in Troy, the Taurus mountains, and the Etruscan area of Italy.

The Welsh (Britons) and Saxons, as well as the Irish Celts mentioned earlier, have histories wherein they trace their lineage back through Japheth. In summary, Japheth fathered practically all the nations north and west of Babel, as well as the Aryans in India, the Maio in the East, and the Medes who stayed nearby in the Middle East.

**Ham.** Four sons are listed for Ham, and some grandsons after them, and a still later descendant who fathered the Philistines (10:6-20). The Bible tells a lot about the nations that came from Ham. One son, called Mizraim, is said to be Egypt. Mizraim is a plural word in Hebrew, so this may refer to the son and his descendants collectively as Egypt; and several of the grandsons named here are known to have settled in Egypt or nearby. Cush and Phut are Ethiopia and Lybia, which bordered on Egypt. From this section of Africa, tribes must have spread throughout Africa and to some of the farthest parts of the world.

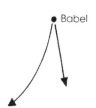

Ham's sons spread southward.

Ancient historians wrote that Ham's family traveled farther than others, searching and exploring diverse and unknown countries. And to whatever country they happened to possess, the children of Ham took the ignorance of the true worship of God, the inventions of heathenism, and the adoration of false gods and the Devil.

A few Hamitic tribes named in this Table of Nations settled on the Arabian peninsula, but most of the Arabs come from Shem instead of from Ham.

The fourth son, Canaan, did not travel far. He fathered the tribes that settled in the land on Canaan and were later conquered by General Joshua. God told Joshua to destroy the Canaanites completely because their wickedness was so great, but some managed to survive by dealing with Joshua or by moving away from the wars.

Ham's most famous grandson was Nimrod. He led the rebellion at

Babel before the people dispersed to their various lands and nations. He was worshipped in Sumer by the name Amar-utu, later in Babylon by the name Marduk, and in Rome by the name Bacchus (Bar-Cush, meaning son of Cush). He was enshrined in the ancient skies as a child in the lap of his mother, Queen of Heaven. This was the forerunner of the heathen worship of Madonna and Child. In Iraq and Iran today, Arabs still speak the name Nimrod or Marduk with awe. (Iraq is Babylon and Iran is Persia of Bible times. Sumer can be thought of as pre-Babylon. It is the Bible Shinar.)

In summary, the descendants of Ham's son Canaan settled just east of the Mediterranean in the land we know by the Old Testament name of Canaan. Most of his other descendants spread throughout Africa and possibly to the Far East and eventually to the Americas. Ham's nations are often called the Hamitic peoples, and their languages are the Hamitic languages.

**Shem.** After listing his brothers' children, Shem listed his own, this time to the fifth generation (21-31). Through his son Arphaxad, the line reached to Abram. Thus Shem is a forefather of the Hebrews or Israelites, the most important people in Old Testament history. The name *Hebrew* came from Eber, who is in this line. Another of Shem's sons was Asshur, from whom came the Assyrians that we also read about in the Bible.

Shem's other descendants mostly stayed in the Middle East, too, and we know them as the Arab nations. Though a few Arabs are from Ham, most are from Shem. These tribes moved southward and filled the Arabic peninsula.

Shem's descendants used to be called the Shemitic peoples. But now we drop the *h* and say *Semitic*. One history books says, "Why do we call them Semitic? Because we used to think they came from Noah's son Shem." Such historians try to teach that Noah and his sons were not real people, but legends instead. Other historians realize that the Bible is the best history we have of those early times.

Which of Noah's sons are most Africans descended from?

Which son are most Europeans descended from?

Which son are most Arabs descended from?

Which son were the Canaanite tribes descended from?

Which son are the Hebrews descended from?

Which son do you think you are descended from?

# The Tower of Babel

The first ambitious world leader after the Flood was Nimrod. As a boy, Nimrod must have heard the story of how God saved his grandfather Ham on the ark. Nevertheless, Nimrod rebelled against God.

God had told the people to spread over the earth, but Nimrod pulled them together under his power. He founded the city of Babel to be his capital. He founded other cities, too, and became ruler of the first empire of post-Flood history.

How did Nimrod get everybody to follow him? He first became famous as a brave hunter. Perhaps he slew tigers which terrorized the people. And perhaps he slew a huge dinosaur-dragon to make the towns safe.

After he was famous, Nimrod became both political leader and religious leader. His religion was to worship false gods, the fallen angels of Satan's kingdom. For this worship, he began building a tower.

Why did Nimrod need a tower? It apparently was an observatory for reading the stars. God had put signs in the sky (1:14), but Satan twisted all the meanings. Nimrod and his priests used their sky knowledge for evil. And they were building a tower for the purpose of evil worship.

Then God looked down and saw that they knew too much. "[N]ow nothing will be restrained from them, which they have imagined to do," God said.

This called for a drastic judgment, to save mankind from disaster. So God confounded the language, and that confounded the thinking, too. Whatever dangerous knowledge Nimrod and his pagans had is now lost to mankind. The very name Babel has come to mean confusion, because people were scattered and languages confused.

All this happened in the land of Shinar. One language group stayed right at home in their cities. Archeologists have dug up some of those cities along the Tigris and Euphrates rivers, and they call that the first civilization, Sumer. Later it was called Babylonia, and part of it, Assyria.

Other language groups scattered in all directions. One of Nimrod's uncles went to Egypt, and for a long time that land was called after his name, Mizraim. Egypt's priests liked to brag that they were the oldest empire. But according to Shem, Sumer was first.

Some groups were not good at starting settlements in their new lands. They forgot God and grew more and more degenerate. We know those people in our history books as "primitive," and some as cave men.

Shem lived through those historic events. He was known as a preacher of righteousness, and while Nimrod was the ruler, he declared war on Shem and his fellow preachers. Most people followed evil instead of righteousness, so judgment came and their languages were confused. Someday God will return to His people a pure language so everyone may call upon the name of the Lord and serve Him (Zephaniah 3:9).

Who led the people into sin at Babel?

Why does the word Babel now mean confusion?

Who founded Egypt?

Is Egypt the oldest empire in the world?

Who wrote an eyewitness history of the Tower of Babel and the beginning of nations?

When the pure language comes back again, will people use it for evil or good?

Would you like to speak the pure language someday?

## Those Mysterious Sumerians (soo MAIR ee uhnz)

Sumer (SOO mer) was late in coming into our history books because only recently have we dug up those cities and learned that this high civilization existed. This is the oldest civilization we know, and it is important for us who want to match Bible history with other history books.

These city-states began soon after the Flood, probably as soon as there were enough people to form small towns. The Bible calls the land Shinar. Abram grew up in a Sumerian city. Sumer later became Babylonia and Assyria, which are also mentioned a lot in the Bible.

Most of the city names are Semitic, but the Sumerian people were not Semites. This gives historians a hint that the cities were named before the Sumerians took over. And that gives us Bible believers a hint that they were named in the original language used before the Babel judgment. So that means the original language was one of the Shem family languages. Through other studies, some scholars have determined that the original language was Hebrew.

Anyway, the black-haired Sumerians came to live in the land. They corresponded and traded with a city to the north called Aratta, so historians think they came from there.

Could it be that Aratta was an early settlement near the Ararat mountains? That's where Noah's family would naturally have settled first. Some archeologist still needs to find Aratta. If you are an interested student, maybe it will be you.

More interested students can translate the cuneiform (kew NEE i form) on tens of thousands of clay tablets that have already been dug up and will be dug up in Sumer. Then the Sumerians will be less mysterious to us.

What is the name of the oldest civilization we now know?

What land did Abram grow up in?

Does your history book tell much about Sumer?

# The Religion of Sumer

Shem was alive in the time of the Sumerians, so they could have learned about the true God from him. But they didn't follow Shem's way. They worshipped false gods, instead.

They had several main gods, and these are known by different names in Greek mythology, in Roman mythology, and in paganism all around the world. The first two gods were father heaven, and mother earth, An and Ki. These became Anki, the highest god. Third was the air god, Enlil. At first An was most important, but later Enlil became more powerful. Were the Sumerians remembering dimly the story that God created heaven and earth and then made the firmament of air?

Another main god was Inanna, who in real history was probably Nimrod's wife. Later, in the Babylonian language, she was called Ishtar and her husband was called Tammuz (Ezekiel 8:14). The goddess supposedly descended into the underworld, and after the women of the town wept for three days, she brought her husband back to a reborn life, becoming his mother as well as his wife. This resurrection story is an early pagan imitation of the resurrected Savior who was yet to come. This imitation religion spread all over the world.

Besides the main gods, the Sumerians had fifty "great gods" called Anunnaki, who were sons of An, the heaven god. The Greeks called them Titans. They were giant and powerful and part human, part god. Some of these were imprisoned in the underworld.

In the Bible we read that angels left their rightful place and are now chained awaiting judgment (Jude 6). Those are likely the fallen angels who came to earth and caused the giants that Noah wrote of (6:4). Giants in the Bible are called Anakims, which is similar to the Sumerian name Anunnaki (Numbers 13:33, Deuteronomy 1:28).

The Sumerian system of false religion has come down even to the present day. People today worship Mother Earth, or believe in the goddess, the Queen of Heaven, or believe and practice other parts of the system. This system began before the Flood, was renewed at Babel, lasted all through history, and will soon come to a violent end like a great millstone being cast into the sea (Revelation 18:21).

Can you see why God called Abram out of Sumer to begin a new nation in a new land? Explain.

How will God bring an end to the world's false system?

How do you think the false system came to include some hints of the true history?

If Shem were preaching today how many people do you think would heed his words?

In what ways is our society like Sumerian society?

# Looking for the First Language

How did language come? Most ancient peoples believed it came from heaven. As late as the 1700s, linguistic scholars had a theory of Divine origin. One scholar studied the gradual shifting through history of phonetic sounds, and showed through this that Hebrew was the original language from which all others are offshoots. He postulated an original pure Hebrew which itself was not corrupted by the sound shifts. (Johann Arnold Kanne, written about 1820, published later in German and reported in *Inquiries into the Origin of Language* by James H. Stam, 1976, Harper and Row.)

Some of those early linguists believed that the confusion of Babel was overcome at Pentecost. The apostles on that first day of Pentecost once again spoke the original pure language and people from all lands understood it.

In recent years, linguists have taken an evolutionary view that by tracing languages backward in history they could find a simple beginning, maybe even grunts. But they find just the opposite. Languages don't progress with time; they degenerate instead. Could this be a principle that was set in motion at Babel?

Even when they study today's languages, linguists find that "primitive" peoples have languages just as complex as civilized peoples. So they are puzzled. And they despair of finding how language began.

Today a few scholars are back to the biblical theory, and believe that from Adam to Nimrod the whole world spoke Hebrew. One argument they give is that proper names before the Flood have meaning in Hebrew but not in other ancient languages. (See "Hidden Message" in Unit III.)

Another argument is that Moses compiled the books written by Adam and Noah and the other men, and he didn't rewrite them in a different language for his people. Scholars know this from complicated language evidence in the books themselves. Some evidences that we all can understand are the editorial additions which Moses made. For instance, in the book of Jacob, we see that Jacob wrote the city name Ephrath, as it was known in his time, and Moses added the name Bethlehem, as it was known in his time (35:19). (See also "Who Wrote Genesis" in Unit II.)

This arrangement of Bethlehem and nine other place names indicates that the books were written centuries before the time of Moses. It also indicates that he did not translate them; they were already in his language. He could leave the original as it was and add comments to update wherever necessary.

All claims that Hebrew is not the original language are based on the assumption that language was invented by man. But no one has yet figured out a plausible theory explaining how man could have done this. So it remains the best belief that Hebrew was the original language.

> Describe what is meant by the evolutionary view of language.

How does the Bible view of language differ from that?

Give two arguments for the position that Hebrew was the original language. Give three arguments if you can.

# *Further Study*

**1. Correlated Readings.** Below are two suggested readings which correlate with the book of Shem. The first is easier, narrative reading, and the second is advanced verse-by-verse study.

*a) Adam and His Kin* by Ruth Beechick, chapters 14 to 18.

*b) The Genesis Record* by Henry Morris, pages 246 to 279.

**2. Map Study.** First, study the map and map activities given in this unit. Then copy a blank map of the Middle East, as in the appendix, and see how many geographical labels you can make from memory. Label Mount Ararat, the Tigris and Euphrates Rivers, Babylon, and as many other cities and bodies of water as you can. Try to show, also, where the various descendants of Noah moved after the dispersion from Babel.

After you do what you can on your map from memory, finish other important items by copying them. Then test yourself again tomorrow with another blank map. You should remember more labels on this second test.

**3. Other Readings.** If your family wants to read ancient mythology, you may dip into a few myths from the classical period of the Greeks and Romans, or into myths from the Norse or American Indians or other peoples that you are interested in. Children's versions of the myths will tone down some explicit language that is objectionable to Christian readers.

After reading, you could try discussing where the myths differ from a biblical world view and where in some ways they retain a dim memory of the biblical view.

**4. Writing.** To follow any of the literature studies suggested in project 3, write a paragraph or essay telling how some elements in the myth you read may reflect real events of early history.

[See page 78-79 for pictures and information about "Giants and Dragons."]

TOP LEFT: Celtic stonework, the temptation of Adam and Eve. Both the tree and the serpent are arranged in a knotwork design.

LEFT: Initial G from St. Augustine's book, *The City of God*, about A.D. 1100.

ABOVE: Serpents and other creatures interlock in extravagant patterns in Celtic art, often biting their own tails or paws. Pagan Celts worshiped serpents, and originated this art. Later, Christian Celts drew less tail biting, but they decorated their Gospel books with knotted creatures clearly descended from pagan art. Did the Christians believe these creatures would ward off evil? Or did they hire too many pagan artists to help them make books? The intricate handwork on borders and initial letters remains a wonder even today.

# Unit VI

## *Book of Terah*

(See page 76-77 for sky map of northern hemisphere)

# Scripture Text

## Book of Terah

**Genesis 11:10b**  Shem *was* an hundred years old, and begat Arphaxad two years after the flood: **11** And Shem lived after he begat Arphaxad five hundred years, and begat sons and daughters.  **12** And Arphaxad lived five and thirty years, and begat Salah: **13** And Arphaxad lived after he begat Salah four hundred and three years, and begat sons and daughters. **14** And Salah lived thirty years, and begat Eber: **15** And Salah lived after he begat Eber four hundred and three years, and begat sons and daughters. **16** And Eber lived four and thirty years, and begat Peleg: **17** And Eber lived after he begat Peleg four hundred and thirty years, and begat sons and daughters. **18** And Peleg lived thirty years, and begat Reu: **19** And Peleg lived after he begat Reu two hundred and nine years, and begat sons and daughters. **20** And Reu lived two and thirty years, and begat Serug: **21** And Reu lived after he begat Serug two hundred and seven years, and begat sons and daughters. **22** And Serug lived thirty years, and begat Nahor: **23** And Serug lived after he begat Nahor two hundred years, and begat sons and daughters. **24** And Nahor lived nine and twenty years, and begat Terah: **25** And Nahor lived after he begat Terah an hundred and nineteen years, and begat sons and daughters. **26** And Terah lived seventy years, and begat Abram, Nahor, and Haran. **27** Now these *are* the generations of Terah . . .

# Scripture Study

**Read** this short book by Abram's father Terah. Notice the details that make it sound like a written record of the family tree. This does not read like mythology or like oral history, but only like written records that were passed down from son to son.

The end of the book gives Terah's age at death. Terah couldn't write that himself, so perhaps Abram wrote it or his son Isaac, who was the next keeper of the books (25:19). Three fathers outlived Terah so somebody in the family must have completed the information about them, also.

**List** the ten patriarchs from Shem to Abram. After each man's name, write his age when his named son was born and write his age at death. It takes a little arithmetic to figure Abram's birth date.

(HINT: For Abram, use verse 11:32 with 12:4 and Acts 7:4. Terah died in Haran at age 205, then his son Abram left Haran at age 75. So you can calculate Terah's age at Abram's birth. From this you can see that Abram was much younger than his older brother and maybe about the same age as his brother's son Lot.)

Add your Shem list to your Adam list from Unit III. Together these make a complete genealogy as far as Abram, and you can use it for the graph project suggested in a later section.

**Compare** your list of patriarchs with the genealogy given in I Chronicles 1. Chronicles has some side branches that you need to skip, but try underlining there each name that is on your Adam-to-Abram list. You should find a perfect match between the Genesis genealogy and the Chronicles genealogy. There are slight differences in spelling, but you can tell who is who.

Luke 3:34-38 is still another genealogy of these early fathers, and you can match these, too, with your list, underlining as before. You may find that your version of Luke has an extra Cainan.

Some people, maybe evolutionists, jump onto this little problem and say, "See, this is not really a complete history." They would like to stretch out lots of time between all the fathers. But this one little difference could have been a mistake of a copyist back in the days when Scriptures were copied by hand. Scholars have now found some old manuscripts of the New Testament which do not have this extra Cainan. Whatever the final answer is, this small problem in the lists does not justify discounting the genealogies altogether and opting for a long evolutionary history for mankind, instead.

**Memorize** II Timothy 3:16. This verse tells us that even Terah's short book is profitable to study.

"All scripture is given by inspiration of God, and is profitable for
doctrine, for reproof, for correction, for instruction in righteousness."

# *Topic Study*

## History in Literature

We could think of literature as having a genealogy. First, came the **real happenings** and ideas. Then those descended into **mythology**. And later those descended into **folktales**.

Let's trace one theme down through the generations—the theme of "something lost that must be restored." The real happening was the first sin, when Eve lost her innocence and needed a way back to God. A mythological descendant was Pandora, who lost the safety of having evils locked up and was left only with hope of restoration. A folktale descendant is Cinderella, who lost her slipper in running from the prince. But with the slipper, he found her and made her his bride.

We could trace a number of such themes through world literature: the flight, the pursuit, winning the bride, gaining the rightful kingship, undoing the spell (restoration), the struggle between good and evil. We can even see in modern literature some diluted descendants of the ancient tales.

The beginning of this genealogy was in the time of Shem's and Terah's books. Whatever worldwide spreading of literature happened before the Flood, we don't know about. After the Flood everything started in one place again. Some of Noah's descendants passed down the true stories, but at Babel Nimrod and other apostates (people who depart from their religion; pronounced: *uh PAH states*) taught pagan versions of the stories. From there those false stories spread all over the world. We now call them myths, but early peoples in many nations believed they were true.

When the nations dispersed from Babel, they took stories with them and thus the literature tree began growing its branches. It seems that some peoples retained the non-pagan stories for a while, as we have seen with the Chinese (Unit II), and such peoples worshiped one Creator God at first. But in a short time the world lost its memory of the true God and the coming Redeemer.

Even the descendants of preacher Shem were losing the memory. Terah served false gods (Joshua 24:2). The darkness of paganism was swallowing the world when God called Terah's son Abram to start a new nation that He would use to bring the Redeemer and to keep alive the knowledge of truth.

So Abram and his son Isaac and his son Jacob guarded the earliest stories and added their own history and passed it from son to son. For 2000 years this nation wrote and guarded the history that led at last to the Redeemer. Then twelve preachers of the Redeemer spread out to tell the world.

Some in the world listened, mostly peoples in the West, and there grew some branches where peoples and their kings began to live by the stories of the Creator and Redeemer. Those nations became more righteous and prosperous and strong than the peoples who lived by pagan stories, and they tried to spread the stories to the rest of the world.

What will happen next? Will the nations fail to pass the memory on to their sons and daughters? Or will they pass it on but call it myth? Who will keep the world from being swallowed by the darkness of Terah's time?

Can you describe what happens as stories descend from real events?

If you have read some old tales, can you detect remnants of real history in them?

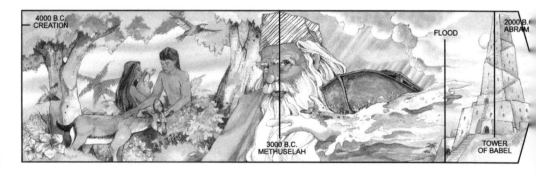

Who do you think should be responsible for passing on the real history?

## Timeline

The timeline across the bottom of these pages encompasses the whole period of Old Testament history. And this short book of Terah covers quite a long chunk of this time. It stretches from the Flood to Abram. No other document from this ancient period has such carefully kept dates as Terah's. These enable us to know exactly how much time passed between the Flood and Abram.

This time period includes the earliest civilization we can dig up—Sumer, which was along the Tigris and Euphrates Rivers. This period also includes the beginnings of Egypt and other empires which grew after people spread out from Babel.

Students and historians can study no more exciting time and place than Terah's, because recent diggings and new translations of clay tablets are turning up knowledge that has long been lost to history. Our understanding of this time period is fuzzy, partly because most historians don't believe the early Bible books are trustworthy documents. Thus when they find ancient references to the Flood or to the tower of Babel, they assume these are myths of the people and not actual history. To properly work out the history of those times, we need some historians who believe the Bible accounts.

The timeline has rounded figures to make for easy memory. It follows the "young earth" view of history as in the King James' and other Bibles that were translated from the Masoretic Hebrew Bible. The Masoretes were scribes who were extremely careful in making copies of the Old Testament.

Other young earth timelines may add about 1000 years to this by using dates in a Greek Bible called the Septuagint. People argue about whether or not mistakes were made during that translation. Anyway, that Greek Old Testament gives greater ages for Adam and his earliest descendants, which when

> BELOW and OPPOSITE: Old Testament timeline from creation to Christ, shown in segments of 1000 years. The dates are approximate and rounded off for the sake of easy memorizing.

2000 B.C.
ABRAM

1000 B.C.
DAVID

1
CHRIST

added together make the world about 1000 years older than in the Masoretic text.

An evolutionary timeline, in contrast to all young earth timelines, makes the earth exceedingly old. On several occasions, evolutionists changed their theory and dated the earth millions of years older than it was dated the last time they changed it.

How would you define "young earth view"?

How would you define "old earth view"?

Study the young earth timeline for a few moments and then see how much of it you can tell or draw from memory. Can you draw the four 1000-year blocks and label the beginning and end of each?

What do you know about the Masoretes from the information above?

Have you heard about the Masoretes before? If so, can you tell some of their techniques for not making mistakes in copies of the Scripture?

How much does your history book tell about the times of the Sumerians? Do you think this is a good balance with how much it tells about Egypt?

## History in Cuneiform

If you learn cuneiform someday, you could read clay tablets from Terah's own city and others nearby. In fact, you might be the first person to read some tablets. So many thousands have been dug up that people haven't translated them all yet. After cuneiform writing was discovered, it took about 100 years to figure out how to read it, and then, not many people wanted to learn it. So if you do, you could discover something that nobody knows yet.

When the Sumerians wrote their own history on clay tablets, they said nothing about hunter-gatherers gradually discovering how to farm and make fire and build permanent homes. They made no evolutionary guesses about how mankind slowly developed language and tools and community life, or

how apes evolved into humans, walking upright and using their brains and hands more than other creatures. No, they wrote as though they knew how to be civilized right from the start.

ON THE LEFT: The word ox is shown in its early pictograph form and its later cuneiform. Cuneiform (pronounced kew NEE i form) means wedge-form. It was made by pressing a wedge-shaped stylus into clay.

The greatest modern historian of those early times, Samuel Noah Kramer, criticized the Sumerians for their view. He said they had no sense of history, no knowledge of the long development of civilization that preceded them. He said they thought their civilization just came full-blown and full-grown upon the world. Here's a quote from one of Kramer's books.

> . . . the Sumerians themselves wrote no history in the generally accepted sense of the word . . . it probably never occurred to even the most thoughtful and learned of the Sumerian sages that Sumer had once been desolate marshland with but few scattered settlements and had only gradually come to be a bustling, thriving, and complex community after many generations of struggle and toil in which human will and determination, man-laid plans and experiments, and man-made discoveries and inventions played a predominant role. (From *The Sumerians, Their History, Culture and Character*, pp. 33,34.)

Though Kramer and other modern historians do not agree with the Bible account of quickly rebuilding after the Flood, the Sumerian tablets do. Some Sumerian tablets are called the king lists. In one list there are ten kings before the Flood, and in another, eight kings before the Flood. Could it be that these correspond with the ten generations from Seth and the eight generations from Cain listed in the Bible before the Flood?

It's hard to make sense of the names and dates in these lists. Sumerians wrote of sars, not years, and we may not have a correct translation yet. But we at least can see that the Sumerians had a tradition of the Flood and a civilization before it, and of cities starting up again, just as Shem says in his book. Here are some brief excerpts from the eight-king list.

> After kingship had descended from heaven, Eridu became the seat of kingship. In Eridu Alulim reigned. 28,800 years as king. [Seven more kings listed in the same manner.]
> Total five cities, eight kings.
> The Flood then swept over the land.

BELOW: Extension of the timeline from Christ to the present.

After the Flood had swept over the land and kingship had descended from heaven a second time, Kish became the seat of kingship. In Kish, Gaur reigned 1200 years as king . . . [Scores more kings in about a dozen cities follow this.]

The Sumerians' history seems mixed up on details, or we are mixed up on how to translate it. But their history agrees with the Bible on the general outline; they knew their cities sprang up as soon as there were enough people after the Flood. Terah's list of ancestors from the Flood to his own generation has been kept accurately for us.

The trouble with modern historians is that they completely omit from history one of the most significant events of all—a worldwide Flood. The Apostle Peter said that people would do this in the last days (II Peter 3:3-6)

ABOVE: A Sumerian king list written in cuneiform probably one or two centuries before 2000 B.C.

What is meant by the evolutionary view of history?

Did the ancient Sumerians have an evolutionary view of history?

Do you agree more with the historian Kramer or with the Sumerians on how their cities came to be? Why?

Does your history book have an evolutionary approach to early civilization?

Today's scholars may misinterpret Sumerian tablets, because they think some writings are myths or literature instead of real history. We need Bible believers to go into the work of studying Sumer. Does this interest you?

If you were a Sumerologist, would you rather dig up the cities and clay tablets or translate the tablets after somone else finds them?

## History in the Stars

The two Bears in the sky, and the Lion, seen on the next page, don't really look like bears and a lion. We wouldn't know how to identify them unless someone showed us or we studied a star map. So how does it happen that people in all times and all places have quite similar constellations?

The best answer is that the star map originated in one place, and knowledge of it spread out from there. It could not have been invented in several places.

In about 1900 an astronomer, Walter Maunder, figured out that the constellations must have been designed by someone living at the 40th parallel north latitude. He did this by carefully studying which constellations the most ancient writers mentioned and noting from that where the horizon would have been for the astronomer who made the first map. He decided that it could not have been made in Egypt or India or even in Babylon, but farther north. Now, it happens that the 40th parallel runs just north of Mount Ararat.

Further, Maunder calculated that the design must have been made in the mid-2000s B.C. That is 2500 B.C. plus or minus a few hundred years.

All this could mean that Noah or Shem or someone at Ararat designed the star map right after the Flood. It no doubt was based on the work of astronomers from before the Flood,

ABOVE: Ursa Minor, Ursa Major, and Leo as drawn by Dutch artist Albrecht Dürer, 1515.

and it showed in pictures some of the earliest happenings in history. There are two pictures of a hero and serpent that remind us of verse 3:15. We don't know the original names of these heroes. But with later names, there is Ophiuchus strangling the Serpent in his hands after the Scorpion has just stung his heel. And there is Hercules kneeling, with his foot crushing the head of the Dragon.

In that founding time of the star map, the four faces of the cherubims looked down like guardians from the four quarters of the sky. Adam's book doesn't describe the Cherubims for us, but John's does (Revelation 4:7). Their four faces were a lion, ox, man, and eagle. At the time of this original star map, the sun was in the middle of the Lion at the summer solstice, in the Bull at the spring equinox, in the Man at the winter solstice, and in the Eagle at the autumn equinox.

The Virgin and her Seed and numerous other biblical pictures were in the sky. Did Shem and his preachers refer to these sky pictures when they proclaimed God's judgments and promises? And did Nimrod and his priests twist the stories to make

From Dürer's 1515 sky map. Ophiuchus below and Hercules with feet toward the North Pole. From the National Maritime Museum, Greenwich, London, England.

the Serpent greater than the Hero? Most early people did better at passing down the pagan versions of the star stories than at passing down the original version.

But we don't need it now, because we have the history of the Cherubims, the Virgin, the Hero, the Serpent and all the rest written in the Bible. We can read there how the world began and how it will end and everything important in between.

> What is the best explanation you can give for the fact that constellations are almost the same the world over?
>
> Who kept a true and accurate history of the times from the Flood to Abram?

# *Further Study*

**1. Correlated Readings.** Below are two suggested readings which correlate with the book of Terah. The first is easier, narrative reading, and the second is advanced verse-by-verse study.

*a) Adam and His Kin* by Ruth Beechick, chapter 19.

*b) The Genesis Record* by Henry Morris, pages 279 to 286.

**2. Graph.** Make a graph showing the lifespans of all the patriarchs in your lists from Adam to Abram. Or if you haven't made the lists, refer to Genesis 5 and 11. With graph paper, you can let one square equal 100 years or any number you choose. With plain paper, you could let one-fourth inch equal 100 years, or any number you choose, depending on how large a chart you wish to make. Down the left side list Adam, Seth, and so on.

To the right of Adam's name, draw a line showing the length of his life. To the right of Seth's name start a line at Adam's 130th year and draw the length of Seth's life.

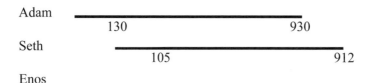

Adam
130          930
Seth
105          912
Enos

Some arguments exist that these records are not a strict chronology and the time period could be extended a little. See Appendix II of the *Genesis Flood* by Henry Morris.

When you get to Noah, look at verses 9:28, 29 to finish his lifespan. Also notice verse 7:6 which tells that Noah was 600 years old when the Flood came. Draw a vertical line on your chart to show the year of the Flood.

When you get to Shem and Abram, refer to information in the "List" section of the Scripture study to figure their birth dates.

Here are some questions your graph should answer.

Which man before the Flood had the shortest lifespan? (Do you know why?)

Which man had the longest lifespan?

Could Methuselah have talked to Adam?

Could Noah have talked to Adam?

Which man died in the year of the Flood?

When did lifespans fall generally below 900 years? When did they fall lower yet?

**3. Sharing.** Choose one of the studies from the topic section and tell the information to someone who might be interested. A family member, relative, friend or Sunday school teacher are some possibilities. If you make the graph, share it with someone too. You may be surprised at the reaction. Many people have never seen early history laid out in this way.

**4. Writing.** Now that you have studied the early history from creation to Abram, you can review what you learned in all six books. Choose a format that you feel will make a good review. One format is simply to list events in the best order you can from memory and then check any part of the list you are not sure of.

Other formats are: an outline, a booklet, a scrapbook, or a written report.

It requires good planning to make a written report covering such a variety of information. You need to decide what kinds of information to emphasize and what kinds to omit in order to end up with a report that hangs together and leads your reader along easily from one thought to the next.

**5. Arithmetic.**

1) How old was Terah when Abram was born? To answer, you need verse 11:32 with 12:4 and Acts 7:4. Verse 11:26 gives only the age at which Terah began having sons, and Abram was not the firstborn.

2) How many years after the Flood was Abram's birth? You can work this out either from the list prepared in the Scripture study section or from your graph.

3) Abram traveled to the promised land at age 75 (12:4). How many years after the Flood was this by the strict chronology?

4) Seven sons are listed for Japheth. We can assume he had about that many daughters as well. Four sons are listed for Ham and 5 for Shem (10:2, 6, 22). What is the average number of sons per family?

5) Assuming 10 generations from the Flood to Abram, make an estimate of what the world population could be by Abram's birth. Remember to start with 3 families (Noah's sons) instead of 1.

You can adjust this estimating plan in various ways that make sense to you. For instance you could postulate fewer, or more, average births per family. You could decide how many generations to add together since they would be living at the same time. For instance, 3 generations assumes children, parents and grandparents are all part of the world population at the same time. Also, you could figure more than 10 generations, to allow for Abram's late birth and to extend to a later time in Abram's life, say age 75.

6) Try estimating world population at the time of the Flood. There you would add more than the parent and grandparent generations to the newest generation, because of the long lifespans.

[If this chronology is not taken strictly, some few hundred years might be added to this period, but not, of course, thousands or millions of years. Arithmetic helps are given below.]

**6. Timeline.** Make a simple timeline showing the six blocks of 1000 years each, with Methuselah, Abram, David, Christ, William the Conqueror, and today labeled as 1000-year markers. You could write your own name as a label for today. Post the timeline on a wall and use it for placing other people and events that you meet in your studies. You could write names within the blocks or, for more space, use columns below the blocks to collect names, pictures, brief write-ups and other reminders of important people and events.

| Creation | Methuselah | Abraham | David | Christ | William the Conqueror | Today |
|---|---|---|---|---|---|---|
| 4000 B.C. | 3000 B.C. | 2000 B.C. | 1000 B.C. | | A.D. 1000 | A.D. 2000 |

Answer 1: Abram was 75 when Terah died at age 205. Subtract and find that Abram was born when Terah was 130.

Answer 2: Arphaxad was born 2 years after the Flood. Add to that the ages of each patriarch at their sons' births. Total of 352 years to Abram's birth.

Answer 3: Add 75 years to the 352 above. Total: 427.

Answer 4: 5.33 average sons per family. (Fractions are okay when referring to averages and not actual families.)

Answer 5: Using 5.33 as the multiplier, more than 55 million sons could be born to the tenth generation. Changing the multiplier to a more conservative 4, alters the figure to over 3 million sons. Adding daughters and parents to this figure would indicate a possible population of close to 8 million as the tenth generation were adults. You could make adjustments as you wish for wars, famines and other harsh living conditions.

# *Appendices*

# *Teaching Helps*

## Flexible Levels

The information and study suggestions in this book can fit a variety of teaching needs. For Sunday school or Bible classes, the Bible only level described below is most appropriate. For homeschooling families, the full study level will usually be most appropriate. Four levels described here show some of the possibilities.

**Reading only.** Read the Scripture text, then follow by reading your choices from the Topic Studies. Or try reversing this: read the topics which most interest you, then read the Scripture.

**Bible only.** Read the Scripture text and follow with some or all of the activities suggested in the Scripture Study section. These require no other books besides this one or a Bible. Sometimes a suggestion in the Topic Study or Further Study sections will add depth to your Bible study. You could add these as desired.

**Bible with history and literature.** Read the Scripture text for a unit. Follow with the Scripture Study items that focus on the content that most interests you. Follow that with topics and activities related to your history and literature interests.

**Full study.** Use most or all parts of each section, adapting and omitting as needed to fit the age of your students and the time you have for these studies.

## The Graph Project

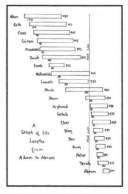

An extremely valuable Bible study project is the graph of lifespans from Adam to Abram. This is introduced during study on the book of Noah and completed in the book of Terah. Children as young as fourth grade can do a good job of constructing this graph. And the time is well spent, since it opens their eyes to many aspects of these early generations of the world and gives them a feel for the Bible as real history.

You may wish to have your students make this graph ahead of time and use it for reference during the studies. To help with that plan, we provide here some brief directions.

A student's design of this graph.

From the genealogies in Genesis 5 and 11 make a list of all the patriarchs with their ages at death and at the birth of their son. This is fun to do as a group, with everybody contributing information but each student writing his own list.

The birth dates for Shem and Abram require special figuring. Besides the main genealogies in chapters 5 and 11, you will need information in verses 7:6 and 11:10 for Shem, and 11:32, 12:4 and Acts 7:4 for Abram. You also need verse 9:29 to finish Noah's lifespan.

From the list, construct a bar graph. List the names down the left side of the graph and draw a bar after each man to show his entire lifespan. More details are in the graph project for the book of Terah, Unit VI.

# How To Use Questions

Though questions usually follow the information, both in this book and in others, it often sharpens listening skills to ask the questions first and then read the information. That way the listeners know they must listen for answers and be ready to give them at the end of the reading.

In a group, questions might be assigned; Sally should listen for the answer to question 1, Joe for the answer to question 2, and so forth.

When a group becomes skilled at listening for answers, try saying, "Today I'll ask the questions after we read. You be ready to answer anything."

If everyone in a group has a copy of the material, they could find answers and read them aloud. This lesson plan is suggested in the Scripture study for the book of Noah's sons, but can be used elsewhere, too. Group members could make up questions to ask each other if there is no prepared list of questions. Writing questions is more difficult than answering them; more learning happens that way.

Individuals studying alone can also use some of the group ideas given above. For instance, they can read the questions before reading the selection. A homeschooler can occasionally bring a question to the dinner table for family discussion.

The ideas above apply mostly to fact-level questions, and they help students learn the information and retell it in the same or a different format.

Some questions in this book require other kinds of thinking or information besides what is given in the selection being studied. For example: In what ways is our society like Sumerian society? These questions can ignite group discussions. Or they might provide the basis for a writing assignment or a springboard for further reading on a topic.

Some questions require synthesis and logical thinking. For example: How does God's promise to never send a Flood again help you to know whether Noah's Flood was local or worldwide? Such questions vary in level of difficulty, and some may be appropriate only for older students.

Some questions are for the moment, to notice a fact and set it in mind. Some questions are for pondering over time. Some questions or topics in this book could occupy you for years or for a lifetime as they have for me and for others who write on these fascinating topics of the early world. Use the questions flexibly in whatever ways will help your study.

# Topic Answer Helps

## Unit I

**Dragons.** Fifth day. KJV translators did not know of dinosaurs or the word *dinosaur*. Create. Some abilities of humans: use language, think of the past and future and spiritual things.

**Day.** The first use of a word in the Bible determines its meaning in all cases except where the context clearly indicates a different meaning. Thus *day* in the Bible usually means a solar day. *Bara* means to create something out of nothing.

**Origin of the Week.** Sun. Moon. Original week of creation.

**The Rest of the Bible.** Yes. Matthew, Mark, Luke, John, Paul, James, Peter, Jude and the writer of Hebrews. It is inconsistent to say you believe the New Testament writers but do not believe parts of Genesis. One who thinks Genesis is myth disagrees with every New Testament writer and with Jesus himself.

**Basic World Views.** God is a person, one God, triune, the Creator, transcendent to His creation. Humans can think rationally to learn about God's creation. The world and universe are real, unified, with orderly laws of cause and effect.

**Myths of Creation.** Small chance that two widely separated peoples would invent stories similar on so many points. When multiplied by other stories from around the world, the chance is certainly zero. The single-source theory, in contrast, is plausible even if we had no Bible history to back it up. Joseph Campbell and other non-Christian writers on mythology take the first view and try to make it plausible by saying that humans had similar experiences (such as seasonal death and resurrection of plants), thus they invented similar stories.

## Unit II

**Who Wrote Genesis?** Root words are from Sumer and Canaan and early Egypt (Moses lived in a later Egyptian time). Geographical names from pre-Moses times. The books sound like eyewitness accounts. Nowhere else did God give revelations of past events in human history. Prophets always said their revelations were from God. Moses did not say that about the Genesis history.

**The Strange Rivers of Eden.** Began as one and parted into four. Mist or dew watered the ground. First and last rivers both flow from a single source.

**The Tree of Life.** Genesis and Revelation. The serpent and rivers are closely connected with the tree in its original history.

**The Border Sacrifice.** Real Cherubims were only at the east border of the garden of Eden. Gold cherubims in the tabernacle of Moses and the temple of Solomon, as well as vision cherubims of Ezekiel and John were always associated with God's presence. This leads commentators to suggest that Adam originally offered sacrifices under the Cherubims at the east border of the garden and met God there. This, coupled with the meanings found in ancient Chinese characters, makes it likely that the Chinese were carrying on the tradition of border sacrifice.

**Where Did Cain Get His Wife?** No. No. Yes. It better fits the Bible facts to say that Cain took his wife to Nod than to say that he found her there.

**Basic World Views.** Some ways that evolutionists differ from Bible believers: They can value animals as highly as humans and let animal "rights" take precedence over human needs. They can value the young and strong more than the weak and elderly, and let the latter die, or help them die. They can kill babies. They can reduce human population by planned starvation or other means. They waste money and research effort trying to find evidence of spontaneous life on Mars or elsewhere. They think rulers should say how children are raised, rather than parents under God having this responsibility.

**Myths of Man's Origin.** Ways in which Pandora was like Eve: first woman, received gifts from the gods, one gift was forbidden. She disobeyed, tried the forbidden gift, loosed evils upon the world, is left with hope. Either gods make people, or matter somehow creates from itself. Both views exist today—evolutionism and divine creationism. Evolution could well be called a myth, since there is no evidence for it; it is simply a basic assumption that most scientists believe in.

**Heroes and Dragon Slaying.** The hero theme is probably the most common in world literature. Christ is probably the original source of that theme; the world's first people heard that He would come to conquer the serpent.

## Unit III

**Giants in the Earth.** Sons of God are directly created by God, and include angels, even the fallen ones who no doubt are the source of ancient tales of demigods.

**Biographies.** Enoch. Seth. Methuselah. Men began to call upon the Lord. Lamech. Methuselah. No. Methuselah. Despairing. Comfort.

**Hidden Message.** Yes. The blessed God to come was Jesus our Savior.

**What Was Noah's Wife's Name?** Se-teh, Seth. Lusu could be from Methuselah. Lama, Lamech. Nuah, Noah. Lo Han, Lo Shen and Jah-hu are Ham, Shem and Japheth.

**Similarities:** earth filled, wicked people, earth convulsed to destroy people, 40 days of rain, more days of Flood prevailing, Noah righteous, made a boat, only Noah's family saved. Differences likely due to oral transmission: Fewer generations before Flood, 55 days after the 40, 3 strata of earth convulsed instead of 3 storeys in the ark.

**New Testament Noah.** Jesus referred to the Flood as a real event, as did Peter and the writer of Hebrews, which may be Paul.

**Sumerian Noah.** The same historians will postulate that the story circulated orally or otherwise for 1000 years before the Sumerians and Babylonians wrote it on stone tablets. But they will not allow that Moses had something from earlier generations also, except to say that he could have had the Babylonian version. The most sensible explanation for various Flood stories is that the Flood was a real event and the source of all the stories.

**Chinese Noah.** True history is lost if faithful people do not guard it. Some who helped guard it for us include: Bible writers, scribes, Masoretes, translators, preachers, missionaries, parents. We can support and help churches and missions that are teaching the true history from the Bible.

## Unit IV

**What Is a Mabbul?** God's promise not to send a Flood like Noah's again should be a powerful argument for Bible believers. What can they say about floods in the world if Noah's Flood was just a little one?

**Ignorant Scoffers.** Many evidences are found in books by creation scientists.

**What Does Seven Mean?** The 7 days, full wickedness; 7 pairs of clean animals, full number to be saved. These may also have allegorical significance, as the 7 years of tribulation that believers will be saved from.

**What Happened to the Dinosaurs?** The Japanese discovery and other "living fossils" found in modern times upset the usual textbook theory of geological ages, by which such species supposedly died out long ago. So, little attention is given to these finds in the press or in schoolbooks.

**Where Is the Ark?** These 3 ancient historians, and others as well, wrote about people seeing, visiting, and taking relics from the ark. There are also evidences and sightings from modern times which make for interesting reading.

**What Became of Noah's Curse?** The curse that Canaan would be a servant came true when the Israelites conquered Canaan. Shem's family brought the blessing of Christ to the world. They will dwell in the promised land forever. Many of Japheth's nations have already shared the blessing of Christ, and Christians among them work to spread the blessing to all nations.

## Unit V

**The Table of Nations.** Ham. Japheth. Shem. Ham. Shem.

**The Tower of Babel.** Nimrod. Because languages were confused at Babel. Mizraim (which is a plural word and may mean *the people of Menes* or something like that). No, Sumer (Shinar) is the oldest. Shem wrote the account. He lived in those times, but probably was not at the tower itself. The pure language will be used for serving God.

**Those Mysterious Sumerians.** Abram grew up in Sumer, the oldest civilization we know.

**The Religion of Sumer.** Paganism was swallowing Sumer and other ancient nations. God called Abram to start a new nation through which He could show His power and love to all the world. The false system will be judged by fire. Satan imitates and corrupts the true; that is, he counterfeits truth rather than creating something new. People who do not believe the Bible or faithful preachers would not believe Shem either (Luke 16:31). We deny God and rebel against His laws. Some in our society openly worship Satan, and many embrace Satanic falsehoods instead of God's truth.

**Looking for the First Language.** The evolutionary view is that man first made sounds, maybe grunts, and then developed a few words and eventually developed complex language systems. The Bible view is that Adam had language right from the start; it was God-given. Evidences that Hebrew was the original language: pre-Flood names have meaning only in Hebrew, Moses did not have to translate the ancient writings from which his compiled Genesis, linguistic analysis of phonetic sound shifts points to a pure Hebrew as being the original from which all languages come.

## Unit VI

**History in Literature.** As stories descend they differ more and more from the original. How about you deciding to be responsible for passing on the real history wherever you can?

**Timeline.** Young earth means several thousand years old. Old earth means billions of years. While copying, the Masoretes were not to change any word to an updated or more familiar one. They devised vowel signs and accent markings to help preserve the original. They checked their copies by elaborate statistics, such as noting the exact center of a passage or book.

**History in Cuneiform.** Evolutionary view is that farming and other skills of civilization developed over long periods of time. The Sumerians did not believe that.

**History in the Stars.** They had a single source. Shem and Terah.

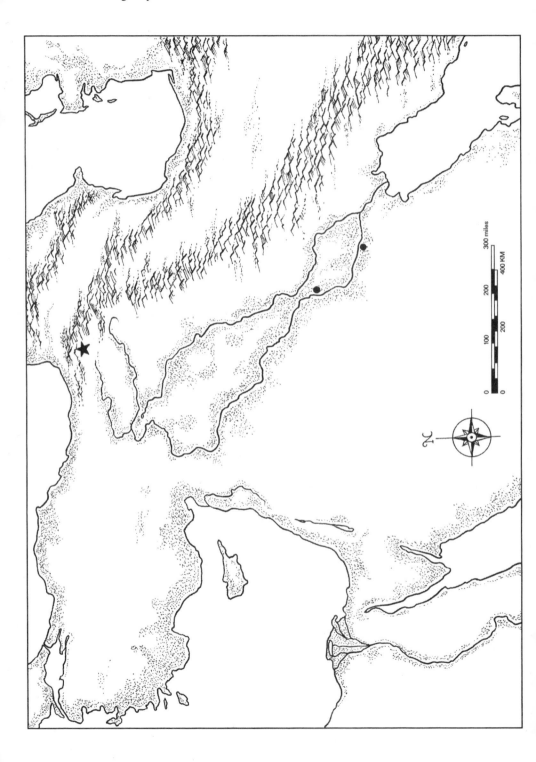

# Glossary

**Anglo-Saxon**     (ANG low SAX uhn) Combined form of English and Saxon. Saxons migrated to England from Saxony in Germany, and their people and language before the Norman (French) invasion of 1066 constitute the Anglo-Saxon culture.

**Armenia**     (ar MEE nee uh) A former Soviet republic between the Black and Caspian Seas.

**astronomy**     (uh STRON uh mee) Study of the stars and other heavenly bodies.

**Babylon**     (BAB i lon) Ancient capital of the Babylonian kingdom. Noah's grandson Nimrod founded the original city and built the Tower of Babel there.

**Babylonia**     (bab i LOW nee uh) Kingdom centered along the Euphrates River, now known as Iraq.

**bara**     (bah RAW) Hebrew word meaning to create out of nothing.

**Canaan**     (KAY nun) Land at east end of the Mediterranean where descendants of Noah's grandson Canaan settled. Known in later history as the Promised Land of the Israelites.

**canopy**     (KAN uh pee) A covering suspended above the object it covers.

**cataclysm**     (KAT uh klizm) A direct translation of the Greek word kataklusmos (kat uh klooz MOSE), which is used in the New Testament with *water* to refer to Noah's Flood, a cataclysm of water.

**Cherubim**     (CHAIR yoo bim) A high rank of angel, winged creatures, who guard the tree of life. The *im* is the Hebrew plural ending, but in English usage the s plural is often added too (cherubims).

**constellations**     (kon stuh LAY shunz) Groups of stars which have been given names, such as Orion and Big Dipper.

**dinosaur**     (DIGH nuh sawr) *Dino* in a compound word means terrifying or frightful. *Saur* in combination refers to extinct reptiles; its Greek meaning is lizard. Combined, the meaning becomes "terrifying ancient reptile" or "frightful lizard."

**epic**            (EH pik) Long poem, usually centered upon a hero in a series of great achievements.

**equinox**         (EE kwin ox) One of two times in the year when the sun is directly over the equator. These two days mark the beginning of spring and of fall.

**evolution**       (eh vo LOO shun) A process of gradual, progressive change. In science it has at its base the idea that matter is self-existant and somehow has creative power to bring about change through time and chance.

**genealogy**       (jee nee AH luh jee) A record of the ancestry and descent of a person, family or group.

**generations**     (jen er AY shunz) Origins. Its repetition in the book of Genesis refers to the records of origins.

**Genesis**         (JEN uh sis) Beginning; origin.

**genetics**        (jen EH tiks) Study of genes and the science of heredity.

**giants**          (JIGH untz) In Genesis 6:4 the Hebrew word is *Nephilim*, meaning super-human or semi-divine beings. Later giants were the Anakim and Rephaim, which Moses and Joshua conquered.

**Gilgamesh**       (GIL guh mesh) A legendary Sumerian king who is the hero of an ancient epic which contains creation and Flood accounts.

**griffin**         (GRIF fin) Mythological creature with the head of an eagle and the body of a lion. In Egypt, with head of a hawk, ram or man, it is called a sphinx. These are pagan versions of the Cherubims.

**humanism**        (HEW man izm) Belief that mankind is of highest dignity and predominance, and rejection of God as the ultimate power.

**linguistic**      (lin GWIS tik) Having to do with language.

**Masoretes**       (MAY suh retz) Scholars of the Middle Ages who copied and preserved the Hebrew Bible.

**myth**            (MITH) A traditional story that may or may not be based on fact.

**personal God**    God is a person who speaks, acts, purposes, and so forth. He is not just force.

**prototype**       (PRO toe type) An original of something, which is used as a model or illustration of something in a later period.

**rational God**    God acts with mind, intelligence, wisdom, reason.

**Septuagint**    (sep TOO uh jint) Means *seventy.* The name given to the Bible as translated from Hebrew into Greek in early times. It is said to have been translated by seventy scholars.

**solstice**    (SOLE stis) One of two times in the year when the sun is farthest from the equator. These two days mark the beginning of summer and of winter.

**sons of God**    Beings directly created by God, as angels, Adam, and regenerated believers.

**Sumer**    (SUE mer) Biblical Shinar; the earliest civilization dug up by archeologists in Mesopotamia. Later that area became Babylonia.

**tanniyn**    (tan NEEN) Hebrew word for dragons, or dinosaurs.

**tradition**    (truh DISH uhn) In history and literature this refers to information handed down orally. Contains some truth but is less accurate than written records.

**transcendant**    (tran SEN dent) Above, outside of, separate from.

**triune God**    (TRI yune) or (tri YUNE) One God in three persons. Three-in-one.

**yom**    (YOME) Hebrew word meaning *day.*

# *Extension Activities*

GENESIS is just the beginning! Continue the Biblical journey through HIS-story with this eye-opening trip through the sweep of ancient history.

### *World History Made Simple: Matching History With the Bible*

Is the study of history merely a collection of dates, events, and people? Or is there a way to tie it all together to make sense? How can students make sense of the "big picture" of history and put the individual parts into context? This book shows how. Using the Bible and it's timeline as the basis for the study, the main events of history are brought together in a meaningful way. The confusion of dating and time periods is sorted out as the flow of history is readily seen in this resource.

This is an excellent resource for families to use to study history together. Because it follows the Bible, it solves a number of mysteries that other history books cannot solve. You'll find the connected and meaningful story that shows God winning over sin. And you'll discover why the Bible is the most dependable tool for dating history. For grades 6-12.

> To help you use this book to extend learning, we offer this outline for integrating this book with the units in *Genesis: Finding our Roots*. Although some of the assignments may be too advanced for younger students, most elementary students could follow along as the material is read aloud and write simple summary statements. High school students should do research projects to add to the substance of the course. The issues raised in the last chapter concerning dating problems could provide the basis for these projects.

**Before You Begin:** Do you and your student need this book? Use this short diagnostic test to find out. (Incidentally, the answers are in the book!)
1. What civilization after the Flood but before Egypt does the Bible describe?
2. What Bible event caused the collapse of the Old Kingdom of Egypt?
3. What Bible king helped to set up the New Kingdom of Egypt?
4. What cruel rulers were in Egypt between the Middle and New Kingdom?
5. Daniel said the head of gold on the image from the king's dream stands for what kingdom?
6. What happened to the image in the end?
7. Can you give an approximate date for creation?
8. Can you give an approximate date for the Exodus or for Abraham?
9. According to the Bible, can we dig up an old village and date it 5000 BC?
10. How did history dating come to be several centuries too long?

## Genesis: Finding Our Roots

Before You Begin

Unit I - God's Book of Creation

Unit II - Book of Adam

Unit III - Book of Noah

Unit IV - Book of the Sons of Noah

Unit V - Book of Shem

Unit VI - Book of Terah

## Books of the Old Testament

Genesis 11:27 through Genesis 23 - The Story of Abraham

Genesis 24-27 - The Story of Isaac
Genesis 28-36 - The Story of Jacob

Genesis 37-50 - The Story of Joseph

Exodus 1-6:27 - The Story of Moses

Exodus 6:28-18:27 - The Exodus

## World History Made Simple

Author's Preface, pp. vii-viii
Teacher Introduction, pp. ix-xiii

Ch. 1 - Creation and Geography of Eden, pp. 1-5

Ch. 1 - Sin in Eden and Murder in Eden, pp. 6-11 (top)

Ch. 1 - Industries in Nod and God's View of Sin,
pp. 11 (bottom) - 12

Ch. 1 - The Flood, pp. 13-15

Ch. 1 - Government Begins, The Tower and After the Tower,
pp. 16-24 (top)

Ch. 1 - Sumer and Egypt, pp. 24 (bottom) - 28

Ch. 1 - Well-Watered Plain, Sodom and Gomorrah, and
The Great Rift, pp. 28 (bottom) - 34

Ch. 2 - Fathers of Israel, pp. 35-36

Ch. 2 - Fathers of Israel, pp. 37-39

Ch. 2 - Israel in Egypt, pp. 40-44 (top)

Ch. 2 - The Slaves Escape, pp. 44-46

Exodus 19-40 - Israel's Wanderings

Leviticus - The Priesthood and the Sacrificial System

Numbers - The Sinai Census

Deuteronomy - The Law in Detail

Joshua

Judges

Ruth

I & II Samuel

I & II Kings, I & II Chronicles

Proverbs

Ecclesiastes

Song of Solomon (Song of Songs)

From Genesis to Judges, the order of the Old Testament books generally follow the historical timeline. The book of Job falls under the time period of Genesis. The Psalms are a collection of songs and poetry written by Moses, King David, and other Psalmists from Genesis through the Kingdom Period.

Ch. 2 - Mr. Sinai, pp. 46 (bottom) - 48

Ch. 2 - Israel in the Promised Land, pp. 49-51 (top)

Ch. 2 - Israel Under the Judges, pp. 51 (bottom) - 53

Ch. 2 - Golden Age of the United Kingdom, pp. 54-55

Ch. 2 - The Kingdom Divides, pp. 55 (bottom) - 57

Ch. 2 - Israel's Kings (Northern Kingdom), pp. 7 (middle) - 58

Ch. 2 - Judah's Kings (Southern Kingdom), pp. 59-63

Ch. 3 - The Gentile Kingdoms: Babylon, Persia, Greece, Rome

The Books of the Major and Minor Prophets look at the time period of the Divided Kingdom in more detail, and how the Abraham's offspring compromised with the Gentile kingdoms surrounding them. These books chronicle the cycle of falling away from God, suffering the consequences, turning back to God, a time of peace and prosperity, followed by complacency, which led to compromise once again. The books of Ezra, Nehemiah, and Esther fall within this cyclical time period.

Ezekiel 9:9 summarizes this time period: "Then said he unto me, The iniquity of the house of Israel and Judah is exceeding great, and the land is full of blood, and the city full of perverseness: for they say, The Lord hath forsaken the earth, and the Lord seeth not."

The Old Testament closes with Malachi's prophetic words. God did not speak to His people again until He spoke through John the Baptist as recorded in the Gospels, the opening books of the New Testament. The time period is known as the Inter-Testament Period.

Ch. 4 - The Kingdom of Christ

Ch. 5 - History Dating

# *What is Worldview?*

(excerpted from *Being a Light: Biblical Worldview and Decision-Making*, by Lori Horton Coeman)

A worldview is simply how you view the world around you. It comes from the German word *Weltanschauung*, which literally means "look into the world." A worldview answers the basic questions of life such as what is true, what is important, and what is the purpose of the individual. A worldview includes one's values, morals/ethics, and assumptions about life. Worldview determines behavior and way of thinking.

Everyone has a worldview. Whether or not we realize it, we all have certain presuppositions and ideas that affect the way we look at every aspect of life. A worldview is like a set of lenses that affects our vision and alters the way we perceive the world around us.

For Christians, we are to view the world through the lens of God's Word. The Bible becomes the basis for our worldview and how we live our lives. Our view of the individual gives us purpose. Our view of the family explains the role of each member. Our view of the church and community reveals our placement in the Body of Christ and our connection to our community. Our view of society and nationhood determines the extent of our influence. All of these views are based on what we hold true, what we value, our sense of right and wrong, and our conduct.

Not recognizing our worldview can cause us to react in the moment, where it is easier to be swayed by the circumstances instead of making wise decisions based on God's Word.

Below is a chart that lists ten main components of a worldview, the corresponding key questions, and the related fields of study. As you can see from the Issues column, worldview impacts every area of our daily lives. To ignore worldview training means we are susceptible to the world's way of thinking.

# Components of Worldview

| Area of View | Key Questions | Field of Study | Issues |
|---|---|---|---|
| View of Knowledge | What is true?<br>What is real?<br>What is knowable? | epistemology<br>philosophy | relativism, pragmatism, naturalism |
| View of God | Is there a God?<br>What is He like?<br>Is He personally involved? | theology | nature of scriptures, role of Jesus Christ, miracles, evangelism, comparative religions |
| View of Life | When does life begin?<br>When does life end?<br>What does it mean to be alive?<br>What is the origin of life?<br>What is the purpose of life? | biology<br>cosmology | abortion, euthanasia, evolution/creationism stewardship, responsibility |
| View of the Human Race and Individual | Who is man?<br>What is the nature of man?<br>What is man's design?<br>What is man's purpose? | cosmology<br>psychology | consequences of behavior, victim mentality, leadership models, role of emotions, counseling methods, heart/mind/brain, disabilities, discrimination, bullying |
| View of History | How do we interpret events?<br>How does history unfold?<br>How does man fit? | history<br>anthropology | progressivism, eschatology, fatalism |

| Area of View | Key Questions | Field of Study | Issues |
|---|---|---|---|
| View of Creation | How does man relate to the world around him? | science<br>technology<br>ecology | health/medicine, logic, use of technology, environmentalism, dominion, respect of property |
| View of Right/Wrong | Can we know what is right & wrong? | ethics<br>morality | good vs. evil<br>moral absolutes |
| View of Society | How does the individual relate to others? | sociology | social institutions, marriage definition, role of family, parental/children's rights, gender roles, sexuality, media/communication, role of education, church institutions, traditions/rites of passage, church institutions, role of the arts, separation of church and state, community involvement |
| View of Law | What is the basis for law? What is the purpose of government? | government<br>politics<br>social justice | natural law, law & order, public safety, crime & punishment, gun control, equality, individual rights, states' rights, Constitutionalism, world courts/treaties, terrorism, defense, foreign policy, refugees/immigration |

| Area of View | Key Questions | Field of Study | Issues |
|---|---|---|---|
| View of Economics | What is the basis for a sound economy? | economics | money standard, markets/tariffs/trade, role of business, role of labor, unions, taxes, property ownership, regulation |

While students may not find the topics listed under the Issues column specifically covered in the Bible, there are plenty of scriptures that speak to the corresponding key questions. Students should be able to recognize that the Genesis study addressed the first seven components. In fact, it is in these chapters that the basic institutions of society were established by God.

High school students can use the key questions for essays, discussions, or debates. Another extension activity is to do a research paper on one of the topics listed under Issues. To get the most out of any worldview assignment, students should research other viewpoints in addition to the biblical view in order to be able to engage others in a thoughtful, reasonable, yet respectful manner.

# *Annotated Bibliography*

Austin, Steve, *Mount St. Helens*, Institute for Creation Research, video, 1 hour. Geologist shows how rapidly sediment layers were deposited, rock formed, canyons cut, and wood petrified after the volcanic eruption—all processes that evolutionists say take thousands and millions of years.

Brown, Walt, *In the Beginning: Compelling Evidence for Creation and the Flood*, Center for Scientific Creation, 1995, 230 pp. This well illustrated book treats all major areas of science as they relate to the early years of planet earth. Students can easily look up answers to specific questions or use this for more thorough science study.

Bullinger, E. W., *Number in Scripture*, first published about 1890s and republished by Kregel in 1987, 312 pp. This great theologian believed that number and words work together, and the Creator could not speak without both of these being perfect in every particular. In this book he detailed his studies of seven and other numbers in the Bible. Scholars who succeeded him often accept part of his findings, but not all.

Bullinger, E. W., *The Witness of the Stars*, published 1893 in London, republished 1986 by Kregel, 204 pp. The classic on this topic, which many later writers draw upon. Detailed study of Psalm 19, showing that God's revelation was first written in the heavens, then in the Word. Proceeds to show, sign by sign, the most ancient meanings the author could discern for each constellation. The originals probably were invented by Adam, Seth and Enoch.

Cook, Roger, *The Tree of Life: Image for the Cosmos*, 1974, 128 pp. Thames and Hudson, New York. Useful for history and art study of this almost universal theme.

Cooper, Bill, *After the Flood*, New Wine Press, PO Box 17, Chichester, England, 1995, 256 pp. Several European nations kept records tracing their genealogies back to Noah or to Adam—the British, Anglo-Saxons, Danish, Icelandic, and Irish Celts. But with Rationalism in the 1700s, scholars had a problem with those ancient documents that corroborated the Bible, and they began the practice of blaming monks of Christian times for piously embellishing the historical records with biblical information. Most books of European history continue that practice today.

But Cooper argues convincingly that these records predate Christianity among those peoples. He shows that they were pagan records kept in lands that knew nothing of the Bible. King Arthur here becomes more real and less legendary. Beowulf becomes a real Danish king rather than a literary invention. In numerous details, Cooper opens up long hidden European history for us. Mind-shaping books like this come along only rarely. It's better to read this one Bible-oriented history book than to read a dozen evolution-oriented history books.

Though the book is about Japheth's descendents, appendices here also give more detailed information about early descendents of Ham and Shem than is found in any other book in this bibliography.

Frates, Catie, *It's About Time*, Dino Data Publishers, Morriston FL, 1997, 78 pp. The likely physical happenings to Earth at creation and during and after the Flood. This differs from the usual topical approach in science books, and tells these matters chronologically, thus providing new insights and readability for the general, non-scientific reader.

Gish, Duane T., *Dinosaurs by Design*, Master Books, 1992, 88 pp. Information about fossils, about various kinds of dinosaurs, and how they fit into the framework of Bible history. By a noted scientist with excellent writing skills for making technical subjects understandable for the non-scientist.

Ham, Ken, Andrew Snelling and Carl Wieland, *The Answers Book*, Master Books, 1990, 208 pp. Answers to the twelve most-asked questions, one chapter for each answer. Some questions: What happened to the dinosaurs, what about carbon-14 dating, the ice ages and Cain's wife.

Hislop, Alexander, *The Two Babylons*, Loizeaus Brothers, 1943, 330 pp. First published in England in 1916. Good research on ancient Babylon and the spread of all paganism from there. Many subsequent writers have drawn from Hislop's work. He proposes that modern Romanism is the Babylon of Bible prophecy. But readers who do not agree with that theory, may still gain much historical information from this book.

Kang, C. H. and Nelson, Ethel R., *The Discovery of Genesis*, Concordia, 1979, 140 pp. The first book exploring the meanings of ancient Chinese written characters. The Noah's ark example, Unit III, is taken from this.

Kramer, Samuel Noah, *The Sumerians: Their History, Culture, and Character,* 1963, University of Chicago Press, 355 pp. By one of the greatest scholars of Sumer. Research based and quite detailed, but readable. Kramer takes an evolutionary view of history. Appendices contain translations of actual Sumerian tablets, including one of the king lists that names kings before and after the Flood.

Maunder, Walter, *The Astronomy of the Bible*, published in Suffolk, England, 1908, 410 pp. This astronomer wrote a commentary on the Bible, touching the areas where he could enlarge our understanding. This includes information about the early times of the world as well as later events such as the' star of Bethlehem. Probably available now in only a few libraries.

Morris, Henry M., *Creation and the Second Coming*, Master Books, 1991, 194 pp. Morris shows how the end times events will restore the earth to its pre-Flood conditions ready for the 1000-year reign of Christ. The two witnesses have power to withhold rain from the earth for 3 1/2 years, and angels will hold back the winds. Thus the protective canopy of water vapor will again form above the earth and men can again live for 900-year lifespans. During other end time events, polar ice caps will melt, mountains will be cut down, and the earth will return to the form that Noah knew it in the old world.

Morris, Henry M., *Many Infallible Proofs*, Master Books, 1974, 388 pp. A comprehensive defense of Scripture. Includes chapters on creation, the Flood, and ancient history. Two appendices here outline information about numbers in the Bible and the message in the stars, which will be sufficient for readers who do not wish to read whole books on these topics.

Morris, Henry M., *The Genesis Record*, Baker, 1976, 716 pp. A verse-by-verse commentary giving scientific, historic, and linguistic information to accompany each part of Genesis. Probably the best basic reference and study book for these early world topics.

Morris, Henry M., *The Remarkable Record of Job*, Master Books, 1988, 146 pp. Job lived during the ice age which followed the Flood, so, writing before Moses and the prophets, he gives information about weather, dinosaurs, creation, the Flood and God. Morris provides a topical treatment of Job's book.

Morris, John D., *Noah's Ark and the Lost World*, Master Books, 1988, 45 pp. The author's own adventures on Mount Ararat in search of the ark, as well as history of past searches and sightings. Also information about the world before, during and after the Flood. Includes colored paintings and photos. Written for young people.

Moscati, Sabatino G. P., *Ancient Semitic Civilizations*, Putnam's Sons, 1957, 256 pp. Originally published in Italy in 1949. The history and culture of the Arameans, descendents of Shem's son Aram; the Assyrians and Babylonians, descendents of Shem's son Asshur; and the Hebrews, descendents of Shem's grandson Eber. The Arameans include most of the Arabs (some Arabs are Hamitic). The main geographical region where all these Semitic peoples can be traced to (by secular historians) are the Arabian Peninsula; Mesopotamia, between the Tigris and Euphrates rivers; and the Syrian-Palestine area east of the rivers.

Nelson, Ethel R. and Broadberry, Richard E., *Mysteries Confucius Couldn't Solve*, Read Books, South Lancaster MA, 1986, 184 pp. Confucious wrote about a ritual of border sacrifice observed in China for thousands of years, until 1911 when the Manchu emperors were deposed. He did not know the meaning of the ritual, but this study of ancient Chinese writing characters shows it to have descended from the border of the garden of Eden, where under the Cherubims Adam and his sons must have brought their sacrifices. Other information of God and the early world, as well as the coming Heaven, can be read into the most ancient characters of Chinese writing.

Petersen, Dennis R., *Unlocking the Mysteries of Creation*, Master Books, 1988, 210 pp. A combination of science and history information as it relates to the early chapters of Genesis. Well illustrated and easy for laymen to read.

# Index

# *Art and Photo Acknowledgements*

Ashmolean Museum, Oxford: page 97t. The British Library, London: pages 8, 10, 44, 58, 72. The British Museum, London: pages 48, 87. Gustave Doré, 1865 Bible illustrations: pages 4, 24, 62. Michael Denman: cover design and illustrations on pages 16, 21, 30, 33 lower right, 34-5, 66, 68, 71, 76, 78-9, 80-2, 87b, 94-6, 100. Peter Dennis: photo, page 19. Phyllis Korrop: Chinese characters, pages 35, 55. Maritime Museum Library, Greenwich: Pages 46, 90, 97-8. Matson Photo Service: page 91. Dr. John Morris: photo, page 70. Private collection: page 22 and cover inset. Heather Stevenson: page 101. York Minster, York: page 27. York Minster stained glass panels, pages 14-15: color photography by Graham Mellanby, painted reconstruction by Michael Denman.

# *About the Author*

Dr. Ruth Beechick received a bachelor's degree in music from Seattle Pacific University and, later, a master's and a doctorate in teaching and curriculum from Arizona State University. She spent a number of years in teaching and curriculum work in the public schools and college education departments, then spent a second career as editor and writer of Christian education materials. She continued writing from her home in the Rocky Mountains of Colorado during her "retirement", before she went to be with the Lord in November of 2013.

Dr. Beechick's special interest in Genesis began in 1961 with the landmark book, *The Genesis Flood* by Dr. Henry Morris. That book has inspired numerous scientists and creationist movements throughout the world which have changed the history of Christian education in our times. Lacking a science background, Beechick pursued Genesis studies in history and literature, instead, and this book is her latest contribution to the creationist movement. She strongly believed that our floundering society needs to return to its roots in the foundational truth of Genesis.

# *More Books by this Author*

### *Adam and His Kin: The Lost History of Their Lives and Times.*

Journey through the world's forgotten years from Creation to Abraham with this entertaining, informative and remarkably easy-to-read book. The narrative form opens your eyes to happenings and truths you never noticed before in the Bible. It also weaves information from history, archeology, astronomy, and other sources into one neat timeline with the Bible story.

Here you'll find answers to questions you may have had such as: Have history textbooks told us the truth? How did mankind learn language? Where did the skills of civilization begin? Why do ancient writings refer to a year of 360 days? What actual events lie behind the mythologies of the world? Who preserved the records of the distant past?

Begin your history adventure where it really began with what other curriculums only summarize as "pre-history." Recommended for ages 10 and up.

### *Heart and Mind*

Ruth Beechick's last book offers fresh insight on what the Bible says about learning and explains the error of modern psychologies. Without a biblical view of man as made in the image of God, psychologies are anemic.

Teaching and learning are more effective when people are viewed with heart—with the image of God within them. All other learning theories view man as simply a body. The body learns by seeing, hearing, and sensing in other ways, but it is the heart that acts upon these stimuli.

This book contains the most complete research available about heart in the Bible. The Bible says the heart knows, considers, speaks, remembers, deceives, meditates, and other functions that modernists like to attribute to the brain. This book also reports physiological research that shows the Bible was right all along in the way it spoke about heart. A chart in the appendix summarizes almost 1000 Bible references to heart by meaning.

By restoring our understanding of the role of heart, Dr. Beechick is reminding educators and parents—and especially homeschoolers—that we are not only "educating," but truly training up the child in the way that he or she should go—in the image of God.

### The Cabin and the Ice Palace

This fictional tale weaves a subtle message of creation, Heaven, and the New Earth while stimulating the imagination and thinking skills.

The children who live in the winter paradise of the sub-arctic world have great fun, but when one of them discovers a terrible truth that the paradise is not what it seems, he must figure out what to do and how to warn the others of the approaching disaster. For ages 11 and up.

### The Three R's: Grades K-3

This user-friendly resource is ideal for anyone who wants to take the mystery out of teaching the primary grades. Dr. Beechick offers years of teacher training and experience rolled up into this concise, down-to-earth, and practical overview of what and how to teach.

This three-in-one guidebook—READING, WRITING, and ARITHMETIC—is tabbed for easy reference. The READING section tells how and when to begin phonics, and how to develop fluency and comprehension skills. The LANGUAGE section shows how to develop written language skills naturally, in the same way children learn oral language. The ARITHMETIC section explains how to teach understanding of math concepts, and not just memorization of facts

### Language and Thinking for Young Children

Jam-packed with wonderful language activities, this book provides parents and teachers with a year's course of oral language study for children who do not yet read or who are just beginning to read. Learn how to turn everyday experiences into valuable learning experiences. Dr. Beechick lights the spark of creativity in the parent as well as the student. For ages 5-8.

### You CAN Teach Your Child Successfully: Grades 4-8

It's not unusual for owners of this classic book to use it more than any other book on homeschooling. That's because it not only offers an overview of the big picture of teaching these grades, but also covers the day-to-day concerns.

You'll find information for teaching the basic subjects of reading, language, arithmetic, history, and science, as well as music, art, health, and the Bible in a relaxed, enjoyable manner. Here's your chance to get off the grammar treadmill, escape boring 20-word spelling lists, and free yourself from endless drillwork that does little to encourage understanding.

This information puts the parents—who know their child best—back in charge of their child's education.

## *How to Write Clearly: The Meaning Approach*

Looking for a refreshing and easy route to good writing? You'll find it here—the meaning approach. With her typical common-sense style, Dr. Beechick explains that the key to good writing is writing clearly so that the reader understands the intended meaning.

That's the focus of this writing "primer"—not rigid rules and grammar. You won't find any grammar drills, either. Grammar terms aren't ignored—they are used as needed and briefly defined in the glossary. Instead, you will find many useful topics and practical examples to show techniques for analyzing writing.

Dr. Beechick shows writers that the harder they work at clarity, the easier it is on their readers. Learn how to link sentences to keep readers from "dropping out." Find out how to do "verb writing" that is more vivid than noun writing.

Other topics include making the message clear, the writing process, how to plan your writing, how to use sentences and link sentences, solving comma problems, fixing sentences, choosing words, and moving and changing words to bring even more clarity. The final chapter offers an interesting account of how our English language came to us. Reading it will probably bring you a moment of clarity, too, as you realize, "So that's why!"

## *The Language Wars: and Other Writings for Homeschoolers*

You'll feel as if Dr. Beechick dropped in for a cup of tea and some heart-to-heart talk as you read this collection of 25 of her favorite articles.

Get a handle on the controversy over the whole language teaching. Find out about actual cures for 90% of dyslexia cases. Learn ways to shorten the time spent on phonics and arithmetic.

Discover what's wrong with the usual timelines and the best way to memorize. Get a heads-up on how children develop and learn in the early years.